RAZEEN SALLY

NEW FRONTIERS IN
FREE
TRADE

GLOBALIZATION'S FUTURE AND
ASIA'S RISING ROLE

CATO INSTITUTE
WASHINGTON, D.C.

The Cato Institute would like to thank the Institute of Economic Affairs, London, for the rights to reproduce this text, first published by the Institute of Economic Affairs in 2008 under the title *Trade Policy, New Century: The WTO, FTAs and Asia Rising*.

Library of Congress Cataloging-in-Publication Data

Sally, Razeen, 1965–
    New frontiers in free trade : globalization's future and Asia's rising role / Razeen Sally.
        p. cm.
    Includes bibliographical references and index.
    ISBN 978-1-933995-21-2 (hardback : alk. paper)
    1. Free trade.   2. Foreign trade regulation.   3. World Trade Organization.
4. Asia—Commercial policy.   5. International trade.   I. Title.

HF1714.S25 2008
382′.71095   2008029683

Cover design by Jon Meyers.
Printed in the United States of America.

CATO INSTITUTE
1000 Massachusetts Ave., N.W.
Washington, D.C. 20001
www.cato.org

Contents

1. A Short Introduction

Not that the story need be long, but it will take a long while to make it short.

—Henry David Thoreau

Western influence on the world, though still great, is declining. Eventually our societies will be the minor partner in the terrestrial enterprise. What do we want the majority to believe about the liberal idea that animated the West's historical achievement and that we continue to profess, but have, in recent decades, ceased to act upon? What kind of world will it be, if the majority comes to believe that the idea is a sham?

—Jan Tumlir

This is a little book on a large subject: trade policy in the early 21st century. It has two objectives. The first, in the spirit of Thoreau's quote above, is to keep it short. My intention is not to write another bulky tome on the World Trade Organization, free trade agreements (FTAs), and other aspects of trade policy. Rather, it is to capture big trends, sum them up concisely, and communicate directly and engagingly to a broad audience of interested readers.

The second objective is to give my account a non-Western, especially Asian, slant—hence the headline quote from Jan Tumlir, who was for a long period of time the director of research at the General Agreement on Tariffs and Trade and its informal in-house philosopher. The classic themes of trade policy, revolving around free trade and protectionism, originated in the West and have been framed by the West for the rest of the world. But the major challenges facing trade policy today come increasingly from outside the West, and particularly from a rising Asia. The 21st century, so we are told, is the Asian century.

Now, for a little background to give a sense of this book's "mental atmosphere" (one of George Orwell's favorite terms). My last book,

Classical Liberalism and International Economic Order, is an intellectual history of free trade vs. protection, as seen in the classical-liberal tradition from David Hume and Adam Smith to F. A. Hayek. The grand, universal themes addressed in that big book frame the picture for this little one. What is the relevance of free trade (or freer trade) today? What is its role in modern globalization? What are the existing and emerging protectionist threats, ideological and material, to open commerce across national borders? Why is it important to counter them? How can a freer-trade agenda be put into practice in the years and decades ahead?

In this first decade of the new century, I have worked mostly on current trade-policy issues: the WTO and its Doha round; FTAs, especially in Asia; and other trade-policy developments in China, India, and southeast Asia. This has been a mix of academic and think-tank writing, consultancy projects, and opinion pieces for newspapers. Through such variety, I have come to think of myself less as a "normal" academic and more as what Ralf Dahrendorf calls a "straddler"—someone at the junction of academic research, policy, and opinion formation. I hope my straddling has been seasoned by the truly empirical experience of work and travel across Asia in particular.

Hence, as a straddler, I lay this book before interested and intelligent readers: practitioners keen to rise above day-to-day events and policy minutiae; academic experts with a practical bent and an interest in the real world; and general readers simply concerned about the issues covered. This book is *not* intended for the overspecialized, head-up-rear-end nerd.

Finally, here is the batting order for the chapters that follow.

Chapter 2 provides a potted intellectual history of the debates on free trade and protection, from classical antiquity to the late 20th century. It is intended to shed light on the big trade-policy questions of today and tomorrow.

Chapter 3 is on the political economy of trade policy. It looks at the state of play in trade policies, especially across the developing world. Then it examines the driving forces of trade-policy reform: crises, interest groups, ideas, institutions, and factor endowments. Then follows a section on trade policy on different tracks: unilateral measures, the WTO, FTAs, and the role of foreign aid. Finally, it sets a broad agenda for further liberalization and associated structural reforms—in a difficult political climate in which skepticism about liberalization and globalization has been on the rise.

Chapter 4 is on the WTO. It covers the transition from the GATT to the WTO, and then developments in the Doha round. It defends a framework of multilateral trade rules, but makes the case for more realism and modesty in a post-Doha WTO. That demands a shift in the focus of WTO business, and changes to WTO decisionmaking. The United States and China will have to lead necessary changes if the WTO is to retain relevance and avoid marginalization.

Chapter 5 is on preferential trade agreements (PTAs). Its focus is on the recent proliferation of PTAs in Asia, which is playing catch-up with the rest of the world. Nearly all PTAs are "trade light" and of little commercial value. They do not threaten to break up the global trading system, as happened in the 1930s. But they are not vehicles of genuine regional and global economic integration, and they are storing up political and economic complications.

Chapter 6 makes the case for unilateral liberalization in the 21st century, arguably more important as a liberalization vehicle than the WTO or PTAs. China is now the engine of unilateral liberalization in Asia and beyond, and it is vital that this engine does not sputter and stall. That depends on a combination of internal and external political and economic conditions.

Chapter 7—the concluding chapter—looks ahead to the next few decades. It makes the case for free trade in the new century. It highlights emerging issues that will come to dominate trade policy, and looks at the role of "governance" at national and global levels. It argues that free trade should fold back into a Smithian classical-liberal framework. The case for free trade should again be made as part of a package of individual freedom, limited government, free markets, and unilateral liberalization. That, however, cannot be realized in a vacuum: it depends on a stable international political order. That in turn depends on constructive U.S. leadership; good bilateral relations between the United States and other powers; and realistic, workable multilateral institutions.

2. Free Trade vs. Protection

The doctrine of free trade, however widely rejected in the world of policy, holds its own in the sphere of the intellect.

—Frank Taussig

All theory is grey, my friend, but green is life's glad golden tree.

—Goethe, *Faust*, Part 2

The two quotes above signal the polar extremes in the debates for and against free trade. Since Adam Smith, classical and neoclassical economists have proclaimed the superiority of free trade in theory. The American economist Frank Graham called it "a ubiquitous and timeless principle." To Stanley Jevons it was "a fundamental axiom of political economy." At the other end of the spectrum, implacable opponents of free trade, from counter-Enlightenment Romantics such as Carlyle and Ruskin to today's anti-globalization postmodernists, reject it on anti-economic grounds. It is a product of the "dismal science" and the "quackery" of economists, as Carlyle put it. It is a bloodless laboratory experiment, they say; a utopia grafted onto the human skin, with damaging social consequences.

The free trade vs. protection debate is not as Manichean as the views above suggest. The reality, of course, has shades of gray in between. This chapter tries to get a sense of where thinking on the issue stands today. It does so via a potted history of ideas. The controversies swirling around free trade and protection are first traced back to their roots in classical antiquity and brought forward to the Middle Ages. Then follows a section on mercantilism pre–Adam Smith. After that comes the emergence and establishment of free trade doctrine in classical political economy, especially in the writings of Adam Smith and David Hume. Then follow 19th- and 20th-century developments.

The purpose of this roundabout method is to avoid a shallow repetition of current—and mostly ahistorical—arguments pro and

5

contra free trade. Intellectual history, hopefully, will give us a wider, but also less superficial, panorama of this central debate in early 21st-century globalization.

From Classical Antiquity to the Middle Ages[1]

Political, philosophical, ethical, and legal arguments for and against free trade have existed since ancient Greek and Roman times. But these are all noneconomic or metaeconomic arguments. Economic analysis—the systematic observation and interpretation of how economic phenomena interact—came much, much later in the mercantilist tradition.

The leading and oldest noneconomic argument in favor of free trade—namely, that it leads to international peace—probably originated in an early Christian "universal economy" tradition. It had a cosmopolitan outlook and welcomed unfettered trade across the seas as a means of bringing about better contact, understanding, and friendship among peoples, eventually leading to the universal brotherhood of man. This was seen as a sign of beneficent divine intervention. In the Middle Ages, natural-law theorists, from Vittoria and Suarez to Grotius and Pufendorf, regarded free trade as part of the *jus gentium*, the law of nations. The 18th- and 19th-century classical liberals, along with Immanuel Kant, made an explicit connection between free trade and international peace. Richard Cobden was perhaps the most powerful advocate of free trade as the central means of ensuring peaceful international relations. That idea carried forward in the thinking of Woodrow Wilson and Cordell Hull. The latter, arguably, was the spiritual father of the post-1945 multilateral trading system. As he declared: "Unhampered trade dovetails with peace; high tariffs, trade barriers and unfair economic competition with war. . . . I will never falter in my belief that enduring peace and the welfare of nations are indissolubly connected with friendliness, fairness, equality and the maximum practicable degree of freedom in international trade."[2]

Protectionist arguments—again overwhelmingly noneconomic— were probably more influential down the ages. Plato and Aristotle embodied a Greek political-philosophical tradition that denigrated economic activity as something for social inferiors, especially women and slaves. Politics was the superior, virtuous activity, the preserve of male citizens in the *polis*. The latter was supposed to be politically self-contained, for which it had to be economically self-sufficient, save for trading in necessities. That meant minimal contact with foreigners.

Finally, much Christian thought over the centuries had an anti-economic streak, with a bias against foreign trade. The latter supposedly inflames the vices of worldliness and avarice. It pulls people away from the religious life, which is intimately bound up with ascetic virtues.

Mercantilism[3]

Mercantilist thinking dominated in the two centuries before Adam Smith's publication of *The Wealth of Nations*, in Britain, France, and elsewhere in Europe. Economic analysis emerged slowly and imperceptibly during this period, though Schumpeter says that mercantilism was essentially "preanalytic": its proponents were mostly pamphleteers full of assertions, opinions, and axes to grind, not dispassionate analysts.

Mercantilism's political context was the ascendancy of the Westphalian system of nation-states. Kings and princes were in the business of nation-building. They projected their power within by centralizing control over domestic societies and economies, and projected their power externally in warlike international relations, not least to grab or defend overseas territory. In the economic sphere, the self-interested, profit-seeking merchant, and wealth creation more generally, were increasingly welcomed—a radical departure from antecedent attitudes. But it was considered folly to leave merchants to their own devices. Rather, the state had to ensure that self-interested behavior was guided, deliberately and forcefully, so that it served national interests. It was incumbent on the state to make trade flow in the "right" channels while avoiding the "wrong" channels. Hence, notwithstanding a ragbag of diverse and often conflicting views within the mercantilist canon, its organizing principle was *raison d'état*.

Mercantilism had at least five main planks: the accumulation of specie; a favorable balance of trade; promotion of infant industries; the belief in an international zero-sum game; and the preservation of domestic stability.

First, some mercantilist writers sought to accumulate specie (gold in particular) in the national exchequer through maximizing exports and minimizing imports. They considered a hoard of specie to be a leading indicator of national wealth. It was also "the sinews of war," a repository of funds to pay mercenaries and fight wars. The accumulation-of-specie argument is now considered outdated, even by modern-day mercantilists.

Second, many (perhaps most) mercantilists advocated a healthy trade surplus by means of export promotion and import protection—mercantilism's "two great engines," according to Adam Smith. Many considered this the leading indicator of national wealth. As Thomas Mun, a leading English mercantilist, put it, "The ordinary means therefore to encrease our wealth and treasure is by Forraign Trade, wherein wee must ever observe this rule; to sell more to strangers yearly than wee consume of theirs in value."[4]

Thus, intervention in foreign trade, through customs duties, bounties, quotas, foreign exchange controls, and outright bans, was to complement a panoply of internal controls on production and consumption.

Third, from Elizabethan times onward, mercantilists favored the promotion and protection of infant industries to kick-start industrialization. Manufacturing was considered a superior wealth generator to agriculture and other forms of economic activity.

Fourth, mercantilists generally believed in Hobbesian international politics and economics. One nation could only gain at the expense of other nations, since international wealth was finite.

Fifth, domestic social stability was a mercantilist imperative. Foreign trade had to be controlled precisely because, if left uncontrolled, it would disrupt the domestic social balance.

"Mainstream" economists, from David Hume and Adam Smith to Eli Hecksher and Jacob Viner, have gone out of their way to dismiss mercantilism's central planks as economic nonsense. A trade surplus (or deficit), in isolation, does not tell us anything, and it is certainly not a good indicator of national wealth. Manufacturing is not intrinsically superior to other forms of economic activity. And international trade, if governed by market forces, is a positive-sum game that delivers all-around gains. Hence Paul Krugman's dismissal of mercantilist shibboleths as "pop internationalism." To David Henderson, this is "do-it-yourself economics." Nevertheless, with the exception of the archaic accumulation-of-specie argument, the main tenets of pre–Adam Smith mercantilism endured into the

19th and 20th centuries, and are alive and well today. They retain powerful ideological appeal.

The Emergence of Free Trade Doctrine[5]

The *economic* defense of free trade, as opposed to its defense from noneconomic standpoints, only got going in the 18th century. In the interstices of mercantilism, several writers had insightful flashes of the benefits of an unrestricted international division of labor, with, at its core, the interdependence of self-adjusting imports and exports, and of trade and payments. Some came close to saying that free trade, not protection, delivers a superior gain with regard to national wealth creation. Charles Davenant expressed this position pithily, "Trade is in its nature free, finds its own channel, and best directs its own course: and all laws to give it rules and direction, and to limit and circumscribe it, may serve the particular ends of private men, but are seldom advantageous to the public."[6]

This turned the mercantilist presumption—that the state should direct trade into "good" and not "bad" channels—on its head. It set up the principle of nonintervention in trade, akin to the French physiocrats' governing principle of laissez faire.

Now it is time for Adam Smith to enter the scene. His genius was not originality; rather, it was to draw on a range of thought before him, seasoned with acute observation of history and the world around him, to come up with a sweeping *synthesis* of the economic system and its interrelated parts. The result was his *Inquiry into the Nature and Causes of the Wealth of Nations*. He drew particularly on preceding economic analysis (from the physiocrats, for example) and his own Scottish-English tradition of moral philosophy.

The governing principle of the Smithian economic system is "natural liberty" (or nonintervention), which allows "every man to pursue his own interest his own way, upon the liberal plan of equality, liberty and justice." And as Smith went on to say, "All systems of preference or restraint, therefore, being thus completely taken away, the obvious and simple system of natural liberty establishes itself of its own accord."[7] Thus, self-interest (broadly conceived), if left to its own devices, conduces to the public good, particularly by maximizing the wealth of the nation. The crucial qualification is that this is not a vision of anarcho-capitalism or unadulterated laissez faire. Rather, it depends fundamentally on an appropriate framework of rules ("justice" in Smith's terminology), which the state is charged with instituting, updating, and enforcing.

Smith extended this economic system animated by natural liberty from the domestic to the international sphere, from intranational to international trade. Book 4 of *The Wealth of Nations* laid out a comprehensive system of international trade, with a many-sided defense of free trade that remains unsurpassed. Smith's contemporary and close friend David Hume wrote some brilliant sketches on international trade,[8] but it was Smith who furnished the overarching system.

Free Trade in Hume and Smith: An Elaboration[9]

By the end of the 18th century, free trade had become the established presumption in Scottish-English political economy. British policy at the time, however, was still largely protectionist; and the political-economy consensus outside Britain still favored protection over free trade. Let us now probe deeper into the classical-liberal system of free trade in Hume and Smith.

Both Hume and Smith made a full frontal attack on mercantilism as their point of departure. Hume's attack was directed at the accumulation-of-specie argument, which he considered self-defeating given automatically adjusting movements of trade and payments. Smith attacked "real-economy" distortions caused by import protection and export promotion in the pursuit of a trade surplus. Both Scotsmen reserved some of their most vivid language to excoriate mercantilism's dog-eat-dog, zero-sum view of international trade. Here is a sampling from Hume:

> Nothing is more unusual, among states which have made some advances in commerce, than to look on the progress of their neighbours with a suspicious eye, to consider all trading states as their rivals, and to suppose that it is impossible for any of them to flourish, but at their expense. In opposition to this narrow and malignant opinion, I will venture to assert, that the increase of riches and commerce in any one nation, instead of hurting, commonly promotes the riches and commerce of all its neighbours.[10]

And here is Smith in a similar vein:

> By such maxims as these, however, nations have been taught that their interest consisted in beggaring all their neighbours. Each nation has been made to look with an invidious eye upon the prosperity of all the other nations with which it trades, and to consider their gain as its own loss. Commerce, which ought naturally to be, among nations, as among individuals, a bond of union and friendship, has become the most fertile source of discord and animosity.[11]

Hume and Smith: Economic Analysis

Smith grasped the insight that moving from protection to free (or freer) trade generates a one-shot efficiency gain: imports replace costlier domestic production, thereby releasing domestic resources for more productive uses, including exports. He then dismissed various protectionist arguments as a wasteful diversion of resources. His analysis was based on absolute cost advantages. What he failed to grasp was the essential insight of comparative advantage, later established by Torrens and Ricardo. This holds that the gains from trade spring from comparative costs (comparing costs of producing a good *within* one country as opposed to comparing absolute costs *between* countries): imports can replace domestic production even if they are more expensive to produce in absolute terms. Comparative advantage, the foundation of international-trade theory from Ricardo onward, points to wider and deeper specialization, and all-around gains from trade, whereas absolute advantage points to more partial specialization and partial gains from trade.

That said, Hume and Smith were much more concerned with a dynamic, rather than a static, view of international trade. To them, the dynamic gains from trade are critical to the long-run progress of commercial society—far more important than short-term resource-allocation effects.

Hume's main observation on the dynamic gains from trade relates to what we now call "technology transfer." He viewed unfettered international trade as a conveyor belt for the transmission of ideas and technology across borders. This allows individuals and enterprises within nations to spot and then imitate better practice abroad, leading to improvements in their own performance and, in the aggregate, to overall economic growth. To Hume, this is a process of mutually beneficial competitive emulation among nations, akin to competition in economic markets. As Hume said, "A noble emulation is the source of every excellence."

Smith's major insight was that international trade widens the geographical extent of the market. This allows a deepening of the division of labor (i.e., more specialization), which enables enterprises to reap economies of scale and increase productivity. This, in turn, feeds into economic growth. Today this is known as the "increasing returns" argument.

Both Hume and Smith—Smith in particular—stressed the role of institutions in linking openness to the world economy and economic growth. The gradual improvement of domestic institutions is the linchpin of the system. Opening to the world economy creates new incentives to firm up "hard" and "soft" infrastructure (to use modern terms). For example, traders link farmers and other small-scale producers in the hinterland to coastal ports, whence their goods are exported. Then come roads, railways, the telegraph, and other forms of transport and communications. Competition from abroad and awareness of international trading possibilities create the demand to improve property rights, contract enforcement, and other forms of regulation and (what we now call) governance. Such institutions help to maximize the gains from trade and associated foreign investment. Over time, this interaction between institutions and external openness leads to capital accumulation, investment, entrepreneurship, and the diversification of a growing economy. Such was Smith's vision of development. His was a model of an open-ended, dynamic, institution-rich economy. Its assumptions were realistic—a far cry from the perfect-competition, general-equilibrium, institution-free comparative-advantage models that held sway in the 19th and 20th centuries.[12]

Hume and Smith: Political Economy

Hume and Smith—again, Smith in particular—fortified their economic defense of free trade with explicitly political arguments that highlighted the dangers of protectionism in practice. Three arguments stand out.

First, there is what we now call the "rent-seeking" or "government-failure" argument. To Smith, protectionism issues directly from the struggle of organized interests within the state. Producers organize for collective action; they lobby and capture government to protect their supernormal profits from being competed away by more efficient domestic and foreign rivals. In excoriating language, Smith referred to "the clamorous importunity of partial interests," which, "like an overgrown standing army . . . have become formidable to the government, and upon many occasions intimidate the legislature." And further, "Thus are the sneaking arts of underling tradesmen erected into the political maxims for the conduct of a great empire."[13]

Hence, to Smith, protectionism is neither a passing, cyclical phenomenon, nor primarily the result of zero-sum interstate competition. Rather, it is a structural feature of domestic politics that spills over into international economic and political conflict.

Second, Smith saw free trade in *constitutional*, not just superficially political, terms. Apart from being an economic-efficiency device, it is an instrument of domestic constitutional refurbishment. Protectionism is inherently arbitrary and opaque: it is all about backroom deals between producer interests, politicians, and bureaucrats—at the expense of the public good. Free trade, by limiting such activity, brings an element of fairness and transparency to politics and government. Above all, free trade is nondiscriminatory in the procedural sense. Protectionism fixes the results of the competitive game, thereby discriminating between people. In contrast, under free trade outcomes emerge from the competitive game itself, buttressed by the equal (i.e., nondiscriminatory) treatment of people before the law. This is central to Smith's notions of the rule of law and justice.

Third, Smith pondered the pros and cons of unilateralism versus reciprocity. Should governments liberalize trade unilaterally, that is, independently of the trade policies of other governments? Or should they liberalize reciprocally, that is, only if others do likewise? On balance, Smith came down in favor of unilateral free trade, more on practical political grounds than through hard economic reasoning. Reciprocity involves incessant haggling between governments; it is governed by the vagaries of "that insidious and crafty animal otherwise known as a statesman or legislator"; it can be taken hostage by interest groups; and it could easily degenerate into tit-for-tat protectionist retaliation. All this can be short-circuited by unilateral trade liberalization ("Just Do It!" in Nike brand terminology), to the benefit of consumers and efficient producers alike. According to Lord Robbins, "From Adam Smith onwards, the classical tradition in regard to retaliation had been quite definitely that it was seldom worth the candle; and while the matter had not been talked about at great length, the general tone of the literature certainly favoured a unilateral progress to free trade."[14]

Hume and Smith: International Relations

With regard to international relations, Hume and Smith were economic liberals but political realists. They advocated free trade, but took as given a state of international political anarchy, that is, a system of sovereign nation-states without overarching international government. This stands in contrast to other economic liberals, such as Kant, Cobden, and later Robbins and Hayek, who looked forward to the day when national governments would be limited and restrained by "international authorities" and "world government."[15]

Though living in a different time and context, Hume and Smith were sober realists who believed that people's patriotic attachment would not extend beyond the nation-state, and that "global governance" (as we would now call it) was too artificial and unrealistic—hence Adam Smith's reference to the wealth of *nations* and his advocacy of free markets and free trade with regard to *national* interest. As he saw it, governments unilaterally liberalize trade in the national interest, and others would (or might) follow unilaterally, in their own interests, when they saw the benefits of such a policy. Both Hume and Smith envisioned international economic integration through markets ("globalization" in today's terms), but alongside an enduring international political system of nation-states. Governance, rather than going global, would continue to reside primarily at the national level.

Free Trade vs. Protection: 19th-Century Developments[16]

The second half of the 19th century was free trade's golden age. In the 1840s, Britain switched to unilateral free trade, whose anchor and emblem were signified by the repeal of the Corn Laws. Then followed waves of liberalization and deregulation that took Britain to almost-complete free trade, and kept it there right until World War I. A phalanx of interests—manufacturers, the City of London, the newly enfranchized and unionized working classes—and an impregnable intellectual and political consensus underpinned British free trade in practice.

It was very different outside Britain. Protectionism, not free trade, was the norm on the European continent (except for a brief interlude in the 1860s and 1870s), in the United States, and even in the British self-governing colonies of Canada and Australia. This was reflected in the world of ideas. Although mercantilist thought was marginalized in Britain, it endured and held sway in Europe and the United States. Alexander Hamilton and Friedrich List powerfully advocated infant-industry protection to jump-start industrialization in the United States and Germany. The German Historical School saw protectionism, and mercantilism more generally, in the frame of nation- and state-building—*raison d'état*, in other words.

Such arguments were political and economic in flavor, but, like pre–Adam Smith mercantilism, they were mostly devoid of solid economic analysis. However, even within mainstream English classical economics, there was, according to Jacob Viner, "a protectionist skeleton in the free-trade closet." Robert Torrens developed the terms-of-trade argument in favor of protection, or at least reciprocity in trade policy. This was later refined into the theory of the "optimum tariff." John Stuart Mill and Alfred Marshall conceded the case for temporary protection of infant industries in emerging, industrializing countries.

Nevertheless, while most English classical economists accepted limited *theoretical* departures from the free trade presumption, they strongly opposed protectionism *in practice*. It was bound to be hijacked by producer interests and invite tit-for-tat retaliation. To J. S. Mill, protection is "an organised system of pillage of the many by the few." And to F. Y. Edgeworth: "Direct use of theory is likely to be small. But it is to be feared that its abuse will be considerable. . . . Let us admire the skill of the analyst, but label the subject of his investigation POISON."[17]

Now turn back to the free trade side of the ledger. English classical economists took the baton from Scottish moral philosophers. From Ricardo onward, they overhauled and refined economic analysis on trade, payments, prices, wages, production, and distribution. On international trade, they paid less attention than Hume and Smith to dynamic and institutional factors, and adopted highly simplified assumptions, moving away from a rough-and-ready but realistic model of the economy to one based on perfect competition.

Despite these shifts in relatively narrow and technical economic analysis, there was continuity in broad political economy: the 19th-century English economists and their fellow travelers generally shared the classical-liberal "framework assumptions" of their Scots forebears.

First, they had a cosmopolitan outlook. Free trade, they thought, conduces to international peace. Many stretched this belief to the point of naivety. Notably, Richard Cobden believed that free trade could substitute for military force and other means of power to preserve the global Pax. Hume and Smith were not so credulous.

Second, the English classical economists vigorously defended free trade in the round, on economic *and* political grounds. Their strong preference was for unilateral free trade, not reciprocity. And free trade was coupled strongly with laissez faire at home; a limited, "knaveproof" state (i.e., one protected from rent-seeking interests); sacrosanct property rights (including those of foreigners); Gladstonian public finance (low taxation, low expenditure, and budget balance); and the gold standard. The package formed a mid-Victorian social contract of sorts. As Schumpeter said, "Free trade [in 19th-century Britain] is but an element of a comprehensive system of economic policy and should never be discussed in isolation."[18] It was a moral and political attitude, an integral part of a wider system of economic liberalism.

Free Trade vs. Protection: 20th-Century Developments[19]

Between 1914 and 1945, the 19th-century economic system was ripped apart and shredded. It was replaced by rampant protectionism, competing currency blocs, exchange controls, and generally spiraling government intervention. The Soviet Union and then Nazi Germany were turned into hermetically sealed, centrally planned economies.

Post-1945, the United States led the attempt to establish a new liberal international economic order. This was an exercise in *partial* restoration. The objective was to return to a world of open trade and stable payments, but with sizable exceptions and "safety valves." There was no intention to return to full-blown free trade and a rigid gold standard. That was because "Smith abroad," that is, freer trade, had to be reconciled with "Keynes at home," the label for greater government intervention in the domestic economy. Finally, new international organizations such as the International Monetary Fund, World Bank, and General Agreement on Tariffs and Trade were created to manage this compromise between international openness and domestic intervention.

Mainstream economic thinking on international trade reflected these real-world transformations. The post-1945 theory of commercial policy decoupled free trade from laissez faire. James Meade, Harry Johnson, Jagdish Bhagwati, and others argued that free trade was compatible with a series of targeted "first-best" interventions to correct domestic market failures. For example, trade protection to promote infant industries is inefficient and costly. Far better to stick to free trade, but use targeted subsidies or other domestic instruments to rectify market failures such as undeveloped financial markets or deficient skill levels in the labor market. But the main point is that free trade was no longer considered part of the bigger classical-liberal package of small government and free markets: it became compatible with bigger government and the mixed economy.

Arguments for protection were virulent in the first half of the 20th century, and continued to have force thereafter. After 1945, mercantilist thinking was especially potent in newly decolonized "underdeveloped" countries. High levels of protection, in the context of escalating government intervention, were justified to promote infant industries, preserve domestic stability, protect national security, and secure better positions in the international political pecking order. Soviet central planning, not the Western market economy, was the preferred model. Like mercantilism in previous eras, this was an exercise in nation-state-building. Milder mercantilism prevailed in the West and in the emerging Tiger economies of east Asia. There, international trade and capital flows were progressively liberalized, but mercantilism found an outlet in policies to promote "strategic" industries.

The climate of ideas shifted in favor of freer markets alongside the breakdown of the Keynesian consensus in the West, and in reaction to the failure of import substitution and other *dirigiste* policies in the developing world. The collapse of Soviet-type economies delivered the coup de grâce to command-and-control economics. Developing countries and countries in transition witnessed widespread and radical liberalization of trade and capital flows, following what had already been done in the West.

17

Nevertheless, protectionism, albeit in muted form, remains popular in the West and in the Rest. Many protectionist ideas—accumulating trade surpluses, protecting infant industries, and securing national positions in zero-sum international competition—hark back to traditional mercantilism. They are products of preanalytic, pop-internationalist, do-it-yourself economics, bereft of sound economic analysis and supporting real-world evidence. That does not make them less popular or less politically influential.

That still leaves arguments for protection that have emerged from within mainstream economics. Several have cropped up over the course of the 20th century. All justify departures from free trade due to the incidence of international or domestic market failures. These have ranged from increasing returns to scale, wage differentials, and unemployment to, more recently, strategic interaction among firms in oligopolistic industries. In some cases, protectionism remains the wrong answer, even in theory. For example, it is better to tackle unemployment through labor-market policies or an exchange-rate devaluation than by slapping on a tariff. In other cases, theoretical assumptions can be narrow and unrealistic when applied to real-world conditions. Not least, they demand high levels of information, intelligence, and competence from government. This is true of "strategic trade policy."

Does government have the knowledge and capability to target strategic sectors and administer the right doses of protection to achieve the desired results? Can it be insulated from interest-group capture? Will other governments retaliate, possibly threatening national welfare gains from protection? The free trader's answer would echo Jacob Viner, who concluded, "These conditions are sufficiently restrictive in combination to guarantee, I am convinced, that the scope for nationally profitable long-run protection is, in practice, very narrowly limited."[20] John Maynard Keynes summed it up thus, "[Protectionism] is a treacherous instrument for the attainment of its ostensible objective since private interest, administrative incompetence and the intrinsic difficulty of the task may divert it into producing results directly opposed to those intended."[21]

Conclusion

The theoretical case for free trade is strong and compelling. On the economic front, free trade delivers short-term (static) gains through specialization according to comparative advantage, and longer-term (dynamic) gains through economies of scale and technology transfer, among other factors. On the political front, it contributes to peaceful international relations. Both economic and political arguments for free trade repose on the foundation of individual freedom—the freedom of people to transact within and across borders. Thus, Adam Smith's "natural liberty" is free trade's bedrock.

Most protectionist arguments are mercantilist old wine in new bottles: they are economic nonsense. But there are more solid theoretical arguments for protection where significant domestic or international market failures can be identified. However, even these arguments, for example, for an optimum tariff or strategic trade policy, almost always fail the reality test. Their assumptions are very restrictive and politically naive. They presume too much government intelligence and capability, and overlook the probability of interest-group capture.

Nevertheless, one cannot help feeling that the modern economic case for free trade, based on neoclassical welfare economics, is too narrow and mechanical, and maybe a little unreal. It is not compelling enough. First, free trade theory has highly simplified assumptions, such as no cross-border factor mobility and zero transport costs. But distance and geography still make a difference to international trade, and international capital mobility (much more than international labor mobility) is an engine of global economic integration. Second, standard theory emphasizes the static gains from trade, but says little or nothing about the dynamic gains from trade and their institutional foundations. Third, the post-1945 theory of commercial policy assumes implicitly that governments can intervene intelligently to remedy market failures. Fourth, and in parallel with the post-1945 institutional setup for the world economy, it also assumes a neat division between what is "international" (the *dominium* of free trade) and what is "domestic" (the *imperium* of government intervention). But modern globalization is thinning and blurring these international-domestic boundaries. Finally, by decoupling free trade from laissez faire, the defense of free trade has been cut off from the general case for free markets, limited government, and economic freedom.

In light of such reservations, there are strong grounds to return to 18th- and 19th-century roots, and to put the general case for free trade back in a *classical-liberal* frame. Free trade should be recoupled with laissez faire: it should be part and parcel of the wider case for free markets, limited government, and economic freedom. Its dynamic, institutional features should be emphasized. Rather than maintaining an artificial and increasingly untenable separation between domestic and international spheres, the links between free trade and market-oriented domestic policies should also be emphasized. Finally, free trade should be seen bottom up, more through unilateral national action and competitive emulation, and less as a top-down product of international organizations and reciprocal bargaining.[22]

These are all elements of a 21st-century vision for free trade. To this I will return in the concluding chapter. But it is now time to shift to real-world trade-policy developments. That is the stuff of the next four chapters.

3. The Political Economy of Trade Policy

To expect, indeed, that the freedom of trade should ever be entirely restored ... is as absurd as to expect that an Oceana or Utopia should ever be established .... Not only the prejudices of the publick, but what is much more unconquerable, the private interests of many individuals, irresistibly oppose it.

—Adam Smith, *The Wealth of Nations*

It tells them of freedom, and how freedom was won, and what freedom has done for them, and it points the way to other paths of freedom which yet lie open before them.

—John Bright (on the repeal of the Corn Laws)

In the last six decades, expanding international trade and capital flows have progressively reintegrated the world economy in ever more complex ways. Policy and technological innovation have combined to produce what we now call economic globalization. Post-1945 trade policy has been a constant battle between freer trade and protectionist forces. Generally, liberalization has been the trend, but it has coexisted uneasily with varieties of protectionism that have always assumed new and potent forms. Free traders, in the spirit of John Bright's stirring words, were at their most optimistic in the 1980s and 1990s, when liberalization spread fast across the developing world and the ex–command economies. Since then, a note of caution and pessimism has set in, echoing perhaps the sober Scottish realism of Adam Smith.

This chapter tries to make sense of modern trade-policy developments, especially the acceleration of trade and foreign-investment liberalization in developing countries since the early 1980s. Its accent is on political economy, drawing on country examples and comparisons to show how politics interacted with economic conditions, and shaped the relative success or otherwise of reforms. This exercise is also intended to shed light on the prospects for further external

21

liberalization in current conditions, at a time when the "Washington Consensus" attracts greater skepticism than it did in the 1980s and 1990s, and when the momentum of liberalization has slowed down. How necessary is further liberalization of trade and foreign direct investment? What obstacles lie in its path? What are its political requisites? What are the links with domestic economic reforms? What is the balance between unilateral liberalization and reciprocity (liberalization through trade negotiations and agreements with donors)?

The first section sets the scene by looking at the global climate for external liberalization, including debates revolving around the Washington Consensus. Next is a review of the record of trade and foreign direct investment (FDI) liberalization across the developing world. The third section probes the political economy of trade-policy reforms. It sets up a classification of the main factors influencing policy reforms and makes comparisons across countries and regions. The following section provides a frame for "multitrack" trade policy, that is, trade policy conducted, often simultaneously, on unilateral, bilateral, regional, and multilateral tracks. (Chapters 4–6 go into the detail of multitrack trade policy.) The last section signals lessons for future liberalization in developing countries.

The Global Climate for External Liberalization

There is less appetite for further liberalization and associated structural reforms now compared with the heyday of the Washington Consensus in the 1980s and 1990s. Reforms have not been reversed, but their forward momentum has slowed. Governments are more skeptical and defensive about further liberalization; and there has been relatively little in the way of "second-generation" reforms (in domestic trade-related regulations and institutions) to underpin external liberalization and boost competition.

This applies to the West, and to most developing-country regions. In the developed world, pervasive agricultural protectionism continues, with an admixture of new protectionism directed against China. The West has no *grand project* for liberalization in the early 21st century to compare with the Reagan and Thatcher reforms in the 1980s, or the European Union's Single Market program in the late 1980s and early 1990s. East European countries are suffering from "reform fatigue" after their accession to the EU. This is also the state of play in much of Latin America, Africa, south Asia, and southeast Asia. It is true of leading developing countries, notably Brazil, Mexico, South Africa, and India. All have their real bursts of trade-and-FDI liberalization behind them. In Russia, liberalization has been put into reverse gear. This has also happened in other resource-rich countries enjoying a revenue windfall, for example, Venezuela and Bolivia. Overall, protectionist flare-ups and lack of reform momentum in the West have reinforced liberalization slowdown outside the West.

China is the conspicuous exception: liberalization proceeded apace before and after its World Trade Organization accession, in what has been the biggest opening of an economy the world has ever seen. However, domestic political conditions for further liberalization are now more difficult. Vietnam has followed in China's tracks, with internal and external liberalization accelerating in the run-up to its WTO accession in 2006.

A variety of factors accounts for liberalization skepticism today. There is much anxiety about globalization, despite record growth across the world in the last five years. Macroeconomic crises provided windows of opportunity for fast and furious liberalization in the 1980s and 1990s, but that has not happened since the Asian and other financial crises of the late 1990s. Indeed, the latter may have brought about a popular backlash, and certainly induced more caution regarding further liberalization. Also, further liberalization entails tackling border and, increasingly, domestic regulatory barriers in politically sensitive areas, such as agriculture and services. Inevitably, this runs up against more powerful interest-group opposition than was the case with previous waves of (mainly industrial goods) liberalization. Individuals matter too: the new century has not yet brought forth a Cobden, Gladstone, Erhard, Thatcher, or Reagan to champion free markets or free trade.

Not least, the climate of ideas has changed, for prevailing weather conditions have become more inclement since the Washington Consensus reached its zenith only a decade ago. There is, now as before, an extreme anti-globalization critique, a root-and-branch rejection of capitalism. But this is street theater on the fringe. Of greater political importance is a more mainstream critique that accepts the reality of the market economy and globalization, but rejects the comprehensive liberalization associated (perhaps unfairly) with the Washington Consensus.

Critics point to tenuous links between liberalization, openness, growth, and poverty reduction; wider inequalities within and between countries that result from globalization; the damaging effects of large and sudden trade liberalization in developing countries; the renewed emphasis on aid to poorer developing countries, without which trade liberalization will not work; the need for developed-country liberalization while retaining developing-country protectionism; and the need for more flexible international rules to allow developing-country governments to pursue selective industrial policies, especially to promote infant industries.[1] Finally, there is the pervasive fear—in the South as much as in the North—of being run over by an unstoppable Chinese export juggernaut.

It is important to confront the liberalization skeptics and industrial interventionists head-on; to defend liberalization to date, while accepting that its record is mixed; to make the case for further liberalization; and to identify the political conditions that might make it succeed. Protectionism and industrial-policy intervention have mostly failed across the developing world: history, not just theory, should be a warning not to go down this route again.

First, in-depth country studies by the Organisation for Economic Co-operation and Development, National Bureau of Economic Research, and World Bank, going back to the 1970s and 1980s, strongly suggest that countries with more liberal trade policies have more open economies and grow faster than those with more protectionist policies. These are much more reliable than superficial cross-country regression analyses.[2] That said, even most of the latter point to large gains from trade liberalization.[3]

Putting together calculations done by the World Bank and Angus Maddison, a snapshot of the developing world in the year 2000 reveals the following. There are about 25 "new-globalizing" developing countries (the World Bank's term) with a total population of about 3 billion. Since 1980, this group registered massive increases in their ratios of trade to gross domestic product and real per capita incomes, alongside big cuts in levels of tariff protection. In the same period, more than 50 "less-globalized" developing countries, with a combined population of about 1.5 billion, saw stagnant trade to gross domestic product ratios and a modest increase in real per capita incomes, alongside relatively modest cuts in average import tariffs. The new—overwhelmingly Asian—globalizers have also seen dramatic reductions in poverty and improvements in human welfare indicators (such as adult literacy, infant mortality, life expectancy, and nutritional intake).[4]

Second, it is not true that globalization "excludes" certain developing countries. Rather, globalization provides an enabling environment that some countries have taken advantage of and others have not. New globalizers in east Asia, south Asia (first Sri Lanka, and now India), central and eastern Europe, Latin America (notably Chile), and elsewhere have reaped the benefits through more market-oriented policies and institutions. They are narrowing the wealth gap with the West. This is why global poverty has been massively reduced (especially as a percentage of world population, and even in absolute numbers, despite a growing world population). Political disorder, macroeconomic instability, insecure property rights, rampant government intervention, and high external protection have kept other countries "nonglobalized" and thereby retarded growth and development. Most of these countries are cursed with dysfunctional or failed states run by venal, thuggish, even murderous elites. None of this is "caused" by globalization.[5]

Third, nongovernmental organizations and developing-country governments have been clamoring for one-sided liberalization in the Doha round. Their interpretation of "development" in the Doha Development Agenda is that it behooves developed countries to liberalize in areas that are protected against labor-intensive developing-country exports. But developing countries should not reciprocate with their own liberalization. What Oxfam and others fail to say is that developing countries' own protectionist policies harm them even more than developed-country barriers. The World Bank estimates that 80 percent of the developing-countries' gain from worldwide agricultural liberalization would come from developing countries' liberalization of their highly protected agricultural markets. It is unskilled rural labor—the poorest of the poor—who would gain most as such liberalization would reduce the anti-agricultural bias in domestic economies.[6]

Fourth, the historical record is not kind to "hard" industrial policies of the infant-industry variety. Infant-industry success in 19th-century America and Germany is contested. In east Asia, its record is mixed at best in Japan, South Korea, and Taiwan; nonexistent in free trade Hong Kong and Singapore; and failed in southeast Asia (e.g., national car policies in Malaysia and Indonesia). In northeast Asia, there is scant evidence to show that protection of infant industries actually led to higher social rates of return and higher overall productivity growth.[7] Southeast Asia's conspicuous success is in FDI-led electronics exports—a result of drastically lower tariffs and an open door to inward investment. China, like southeast Asia, has grown fast through FDI-led exports, not infant-industry protection. Arguably, other factors—political and macroeconomic stability, competitive exchange rates, private property rights, openness to the world economy, education, and infrastructure—were much more important to east Asian success than "picking winners."

Finally, infant-industry protection in Latin America, south Asia, and Africa has been a disaster not dissimilar to industrial planning in ex–command economies. Protected infants sooner or later ran into severe problems, and governments continued to subsidize and protect perpetual children. Such incestuous government-business links provided a fertile breeding ground for corruption. Besides, most developing-country markets are too small to support infant-industry promotion, and their states are too weak, incompetent, and corrupt to efficiently administer the complex instruments required.

Protectionism in the World: Unfinished Business

Protectionism remains high around the world, even after six decades of liberalization, first in developed countries and then in developing countries. There are pockets of developed-country protection—agricultural subsidies, peak tariffs and tariff escalation in agriculture and manufactures, anti-dumping duties, assorted regulatory barriers such as onerous product standards, and high restrictions on the cross-border movement of workers—that continue to damage developing-country growth prospects.

But developing countries' own protection on almost all these counts is much higher and more damaging. Average applied tariffs in developing countries are more than double those in developed countries, with much higher bound rates in the WTO (Table 3.1). South Asia, sub-Saharan Africa, the Middle East, and North Africa have higher average tariffs than east Asia, Latin America, and eastern Europe (Table 3.2). Bound and applied tariffs in agriculture are significantly higher than they are in manufactures. Developing countries have become bigger users of anti-dumping actions than developed countries (Figure 3.1). A few developing countries—notably

Table 3.1
BOUND AND APPLIED TARIFF RATES

	Bound %		Applied %	
	Developed economies	Developing economies	Developed economies	Developing economies
All goods	17.8	43.6	5.5	11.8
Agriculture	24.3	60.6	9.5	16.3
Manufactures	16.7	32.5	4.8	11.0

SOURCE: World Bank trade databases: http://siteresources.worldbank.org/ INTRES/Resources/469232-1107449512766/tar2005a.xls.

NOTE: Developed and developing economies by World Bank definitions. Developed economies: category 3–4 (2002–2004), Developing economies: category 1–2 (1998–2004).

Table 3.2
TARIFF RATES IN DIFFERENT REGIONS

Country group or region	Applied	Bound	Agriculture (applied)	Manufactures (applied)
High-income economies	5.5	17.8	10.6	3.3
Latin America and the Caribbean	9.9	41.2	14.9	9.0
East Asia and Pacific	10.5	29.5	16.8	10.5
South Asia	17.8	66.5	19.1	17.2
Europe and Central Asia	7.8	13.2	14.0	6.7
Middle East and North Africa	18.0	34.6	22.5	16.9
Sub-Saharan Africa	13.4	61.5	17.2	12.9

SOURCE: World Bank trade databases: http://siteresources.worldbank.org/ INTRES/Resources/469232-1107449512766/tar2005a.xls.

NOTE: The numbers are unweighted averages in percents from 1998 to 2004. Regional definitions by the World Bank: http://web.worldbank.org/ WBSITE/EXTERNAL/DATASTATISTICS/0,,contentMDK:20421402~page PK:64133150~piPK:64133175~theSitePK:239419,00.html.

Figure 3.1
ANTI-DUMPING MEASURES, 1995–2000

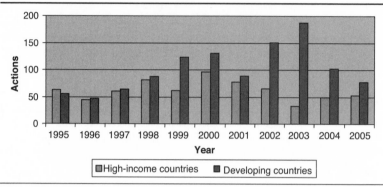

SOURCE: WTO, www.wto.org/english/tratop_e/adp_e/adp_stattab7_e.xls.

NOTE: Anti-dumping measures by reporting member. Classification of countries by World Bank definitions.

Figure 3.2
MOST FREQUENT USERS OF ANTI-DUMPING MEASURES, 1995–2000

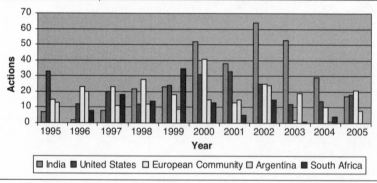

SOURCE: WTO, www.wto.org/english/tratop_e/adp_e/adp_stattab7_e.xls.

NOTE: Anti-dumping measures by reporting member.

India—have become much more frequent users of anti-dumping actions (Figure 3.2). With the exception of countries in transition and those that have recently acceded to the WTO, developing countries have far fewer multilateral commitments than developed countries in services (Figure 3.3). There has been a general increase in

Figure 3.3
Distribution of GATS Commitments Across Groups of
Members, March 2005 (Average number of subsectors
committed per member)

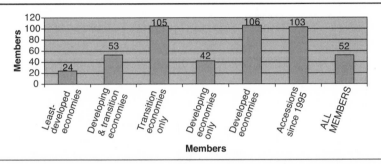

SOURCE: R.Adlung and M. Roy, "Turning Hills Into Mountains? Current Commitments under the GATS and Prospects for Change," Staff Working Paper ERSD-2005-01, WTO, Geneva, March 2005, www.wto.org/english/res_e/reser_e/ersd200501_e.doc.

the use of technical, food-safety, and other standards that affect trade, as indicated by the number of measures notified under the WTO's Technical Barriers to Trade and Sanitary and Phytosanitary Agreements. This is one—admittedly very rough—indication of regulatory barriers to trade. Developed countries account for over half of technical barriers to trade and sanitary and phytosanitary measures notified, but what is also striking is the increasing number of measures notified by developing countries (Figures 3.4 and 3.5).

Thus, there is much unfinished business with regard to liberalizing trade, capital flows, and the cross-border movement of labor in the developing world. That said, external liberalization is no panacea. In the short run, trade liberalization reduces the anti-import, anti-export bias of trade taxes. That is the prelude to dynamic gains— including those from trade-related inward investment—that result in productivity improvements and growth. Capturing these gains, however, depends on additional factors: initial conditions for reform, including a country's factor endowments and historical legacy; complementary domestic market-based reforms; and the state of and improvement in domestic institutions. The connection between opening to the world economy and domestic economic and institutional reform is particularly important: it is this that explains much

Figure 3.4
NUMBER OF NOTIFIED SANITARY AND PHYTOSANITARY MEASURES,
1995–2001

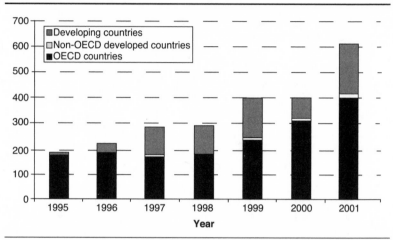

SOURCE: "Sanitary and Phytosanitary Measures and Agricultural Trade: A Survey of Issues and Concerns Raised in the WTO's SPS Committee," COM/TD/AGR/WP(2002)21/FINAL, OECD, Paris, July 5, 2002, www.olis.oecd.org/olis/2002doc.nsf/43bb6130e5e86e5fc12569fa005d004c/7b8815fac33fe88ec1256bed002e5cb7/$FILE/JT00129244.PDF.

of the variation in economic performance in the developing world. As I argued in the last chapter, this is not a new insight: David Hume and Adam Smith strongly linked free trade (broadly defined to include cross-border flows of capital and people) to domestic institutions and growth, all on the canvas of the long-run progress of commercial society. But this also begs difficult political questions. In essence, successful external opening depends crucially on domestic politics and institutional capacity. Here, there are very large and arguably increasing differences within the developing world.

Trade-Policy Reforms: The Recent Experience, with Country Examples

Trade liberalization has several definitions. Trade economists speak of moving to "neutrality" of government intervention as between tradable and nontradable sectors of the economy. They also speak of "getting prices right" by aligning domestic prices with

Figure 3.5
NUMBER OF NOTIFIED TECHNICAL BARRIERS TO TRADE MEASURES,
1995–2001

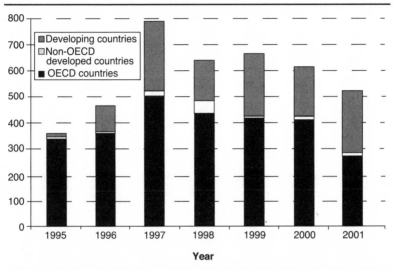

SOURCE: "Agro-Food Products and Technical Barriers to Trade: A Survey of Issues and Concerns Raised in the WTO's TBT Committee," COM/TD/AGR/WP(2002)70/FINAL, OECD, Paris, March 4, 2003, www.olis.oecd.org/olis/2002doc.nsf/43bb6130e5e86e5fc12569fa005d004c/baacb7d0229000f9c1256cdf00418c0f/$FILE/JT00140246.PDF.

world prices of tradable goods. More broadly conceived, free (or freeish) trade means the freedom to engage in international transactions, without discrimination.[8] This exists nowhere—not even in Hong Kong, which maintains tight restrictions on immigration, though it is fully open to trade in goods and capital flows, and largely open to trade in services. If nondiscrimination is the relevant criterion, all countries are still far from free trade, indeed more so than was the case in the late 19th century.

Nevertheless, there has been a distinct liberalization trend in developing countries in recent decades.[9] Cross-border trade and capital flows—though not of people—have become freer. There is less discrimination between domestic and international transactions. Domestic prices of tradable goods and services are closer to world prices (though less the case in services than in goods). With regard to measures undertaken, import and export quotas, licenses, state trading monopolies, and other nontariff barriers have been drastically reduced. Tariffs have been simplified and reduced. So have foreign-exchange controls, with unified exchange rates and much greater currency convertibility, especially on current-account transactions. Foreign direct investment has been liberalized, with fewer restrictions on entry, ownership, establishment, and operation in the domestic economy. And services sectors have been opened to international competition through FDI liberalization, privatization, and domestic deregulation. Overall, trade and FDI in manufactured goods have been liberalized most; trade and FDI in services were liberalized later, and to a much lesser extent; and trade liberalization in agriculture has lagged behind. Finally, trade and FDI liberalization have taken place in the context of wide-ranging macro- and microeconomic market-based reforms—roughly the "stabilization and liberalization" package of the Washington Consensus, as described by John Williamson.

Cumulatively, this has been a veritable policy revolution in developing countries and countries in transition. Before the 1980s, the 80 percent of the world's population then living outside the West lived overwhelmingly in countries with high levels of external protection, in addition to pervasive government intervention at home. By the mid-1990s, most of these people lived in much more open economies, in both domestic and international commerce. Average applied tariffs in developing countries declined from 30 percent in 1985 to 11 percent in 2005 (Figure 3.6). Core nontariff barriers declined correspondingly in all developing-country regions (Table 3.3). The bulk of regulatory changes on inward investment has been more favorable to FDI (Table 3.4). There has even been a trend in favor of capital-account liberalization: 70 percent of the developing countries in the International Monetary Fund maintain capital-account restrictions today, compared with 85 percent in the early 1990s (Figure 3.7).

This liberalization trend started in Japan, and then South Korea and Taiwan, in the 1950s and 1960s, at a time when most developing countries were tightening regimes of import substitution and other forms of state intervention. The northeast Asian Tigers promoted exports through selective liberalization, while retaining considerable import protection and restrictions on inward investment. Later, they gradually liberalized imports and FDI. Hong Kong returned to tariff-free trade and a fully open door to investment after the war. Singapore

Table 3.3
FREQUENCY OF NONTARIFF BARRIERS IN DEVELOPING COUNTRIES,
1989–2000 (PERCENT)

Region	1989–94	1995–98	2000
East Asia and the Pacific	30.1	16.3	5.5
Latin America and the Caribbean	18.3	8.0	15.3
Middle East and North Africa	43.8	16.6	8.5
South Asia	57.0	58.3	13.3
Sub-Saharan Africa	26.0	10.4	2.3

SOURCES: For 1989–94 and 1995–98: "Dealing with the Revenue Consequences of Trade Reform," IMF, Washington, DC, February 15, 2005, www.imf.org/external/np/pp/eng/2005/021505.pdf, citing B. Hoekman, "Economic Development and the WTO after Doha," Policy Research Working Paper 2851, World Bank, Washington, DC, June 2002; for 2000: Cordell Institute, www.cordellhullinstitute.org/TPA/Volume%207%20(2005)/Vol%207,%20 No.%202%20-%20Thomas%20Dalsgaard%20on%20Trade%20Reform% 20&%20Revenue%20Loss.pdf, citing World Bank, "Global Monitoring Report," Washington, DC, 2004, table 4.6.

NOTE: Figures are regional averages of percentage of tariff lines subject to core NTBs, including all types of quantity restrictions and price administration or control, as well as monopolistic trading channels.

followed, though after a brief flirtation with protection (when part of the Federation of Malaysia). The other southeast Asian Tigers (Malaysia, Thailand, Indonesia, and the Philippines) liberalized significantly, on both trade and FDI, from the 1970s. The countries of Indochina started gradual and halting market-based reforms in the 1980s. Vietnam accelerated trade-and-investment liberalization in the run-up to its WTO accession in late 2006.

China's historic opening dates back to 1978, but major trade-and-investment liberalization took off from the early 1990s. Since then, China has swung from extreme protection to rather liberal trade policies, indeed very liberal by developing-country standards. The crowning point of China's reforms was its WTO accession in 2001. Its WTO commitments are by far the strongest of any developing country in the WTO.

In south Asia, Sri Lanka pioneered external liberalization in the late 1970s. India's retreat from the "license raj"—its equivalent of Soviet-style central planning—began half-heartedly in the 1980s,

Table 3.4
NATIONAL REGULATORY CHANGES ON FDI, 1992–2005, BY REGION

Region	Changes	1992	1993	1994	1995	1996	1997	1998	1999	2000	2001	2002	2003	2004	2005
World	More favorable	77	99	108	106	98	134	136	130	147	193	234	218	234	164
	Less favorable	—	1	2	6	16	16	9	9	3	14	12	24	36	41
Developed countries	More favorable	11	24	17	22	25	36	20	27	29	38	54	45	54	40
	Less favorable	—	—	1	2	3	6	4	5	—	3	2	3	6	4
Developing countries	More favorable	49	63	79	62	58	87	109	78	105	127	144	139	144	92
	Less favorable	—	1	1	3	10	5	3	2	2	10	9	20	27	30
Africa	More favorable	9	12	22	12	15	14	23	16	13	25	21	43	46	42
	Less favorable	—	—	—	—	2	—	1	—	—	3	6	2	11	11
Latin America and the Caribbean	More favorable	9	17	14	18	14	30	13	17	29	18	15	16	26	7
	Less favorable	—	—	—	2	1	4	2	2	—	3	2	11	9	14
West Asia	More favorable	3	8	4	4	4	5	18	7	24	26	34	35	34	15
	Less favorable	—	—	—	—	—	—	—	—	1	2	1	4	1	1
South, east, and southeast Asia	More favorable	27	26	39	28	25	33	52	37	38	58	74	44	37	28
	Less favorable	—	1	1	1	7	1	—	—	1	2	—	3	6	4
Oceania	More favorable	1	—	—	—	—	5	3	1	1	—	—	—	1	—

SOURCE: UNCTAD, Reference Thomas Pollan (Economic Affairs Officer).
— = Not available.

Figure 3.6
AVERAGE APPLIED TARIFF RATES IN DEVELOPING COUNTRIES,
1981–2005 (Unweighted in %)

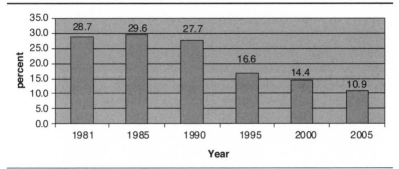

SOURCE: World Bank trade databases: http://siteresources.worldbank.org/
INTRES/Resources/tar2005.xls.

but its decisive opening to the world economy dates back to 1991. Pakistan followed in the late 1990s.

In Latin America, Chile pioneered radical external liberalization in the 1970s. Other Latin American countries followed in the 1980s (notably Mexico) and 1990s (notably Brazil, Argentina, and Peru). African liberalization was slow in the 1980s and faster in the 1990s. South Africa had a big opening of the economy in the run-up to and after the end of apartheid. The countries of east-central Europe and the Baltic States had a "big bang" transition from the Plan to the Market after 1989, which included massive liberalization of trade and capital flows. This was less the case, and certainly more erratic, in Russia, other parts of the ex–Soviet Union, and southeastern Europe. However, liberalization has recently accelerated in some of these countries, for example, Romania, Bulgaria, Georgia, and parts of the ex-Yugoslavia.

Finally, trade-and-investment liberalization in the old Organisation for Economic Co-operation and Development countries has taken place in small steps since the 1980s—not surprising, since these are largely open economies in which the bulk of liberalization was done in the 1950s and 1960s. The exceptions are Australia and New Zealand. After more than a century of protection, both opened decisively to the world economy in the 1980s.

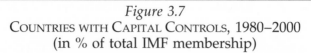

Figure 3.7
COUNTRIES WITH CAPITAL CONTROLS, 1980–2000
(in % of total IMF membership)

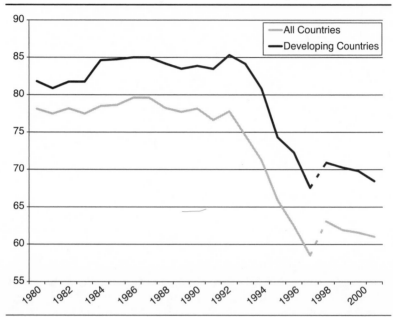

Based on a simple 1–0 classification (covering all capital account transactions), as provided by the AREAER. There was a definitional change from 1997 to 1998.

SOURCE: International Monetary Fund, *The IMF's Approach to Capital Account Liberalization: Evaluation Report*, The IMF Independent Evaluation Office, Washington, DC, 2005, p. 12: www.imf.org/external/np/ieo/2005/cal/eng/report.pdf.

Political Economy and Trade-Policy Reforms

The politics of economic-policy reform is as much about distribution as it is about wealth generation. This is true of international politics; it is even truer of domestic politics. Shifts in trade policy—from protection to openness or vice versa—trigger redistribution of gains and losses between regions (especially between rural and urban areas); sectors of the economy (agriculture, industry, and services); classes (owners of capital, educated and skilled workers, and semi- and unskilled workers); and even between ethnic groups.

Such disruption, especially in the short term, can be particularly unsettling in developing countries with political instability, corrupt elites, wide disparities in wealth and influence, meager safety nets, ethnic divides, and generally brittle institutions. Hence, trade and other forms of liberalization take place in a snake pit of messy and sometimes poisonous politics.

What are the determinants of trade-policy reform, especially in the direction of liberalization? What follows is a simple taxonomy of relevant factors: (a) circumstances, especially crises; (b) interests; (c) ideas; (d) institutions; and (e) factor endowments.

Circumstances/Crises

> *Events, dear boy, events.*
>
> —Harold Macmillan

> *When a man knows he is going to be hanged in a fortnight, it concentrates the mind wonderfully.*
>
> —Dr. Johnson

The practical politician, official, or businessperson knows that choices are dictated by responses to often-unanticipated events. In reality, major episodes of economic-policy reform have mostly taken place in response to political or economic crises, or both. A macroeconomic crisis, with symptoms such as extreme internal or external indebtedness, hyperinflation, a terms-of-trade shock, or a severe payments imbalance leading to a plummeting currency, provides the classic backdrop. This is when "normal politics" is suspended, and when a period of "extraordinary politics" can provide a window of opportunity for thoroughgoing reforms (that would not be possible in "normal" political circumstances).[10] Examples are legion: Chile in 1973–94; Mexico in 1986; Brazil and Argentina in the early 1990s; South Africa in the mid-1990s; Sri Lanka in 1977; India in 1991; eastern Europe and the ex–Soviet Union in the early 1990s; and Australia and New Zealand in 1983–84.

But the crisis explanation cannot be taken too far. First, a crisis can precipitate swings both ways: sometimes toward liberalization; sometimes the other way, as happened during the Depression in the 1930s and, to a lesser extent, in the 1970s after the first oil-price shock. Second, different governments act in different ways in response to similar external shocks. Third, a crisis might trigger some reforms, but it is no guarantee of the sustainability of those reforms, nor of further reforms down the line. That is one key difference between east-central Europe and the Baltic States, on the one hand, and Russia and other parts of the ex–Soviet Union, on the other. Fourth, there are counterexamples of gradual, but cumulatively substantial, reforms without a sudden crisis as a triggering mechanism. That is, roughly, the east Asian record.

Why have some countries sustained reforms while others have not? Why have some gone further than others? What happens to a reform program postcrisis, when "normal" political and economic conditions return? These questions demand supplementary explanations.

Interests

> *A good cause seldom triumphs without someone's interest behind it.*
>
> —John Stuart Mill

Mainstream economists, following Adam Smith, tend to rely on an interest-group explanation of trade politics. Free trade is the optimal policy in most circumstances (they say), but protection more often the result, because organized rent-seeking interests demand protection, and politicians and officials supply it. The benefits of free trade are diffused over the broad majority of consumers, but its costs bear down disproportionately on minority producer interests. The latter, not the former, have the incentive to organize for collective action.[11] In reality, "iron quadrangles" of politicians, bureaucrats, employers, and unions imposed a straightjacket of protection in developing countries from the 1930s to the 1970s. Mostly this benefited capital-intensive, unionized, urban manufacturing industries producing for the domestic market, at the expense of agriculture and tradable sectors. India's license raj was its most notorious incarnation. In many countries, a crisis was used to overcome interest-group opposition and push through liberalizing reforms (as happened in India in 1991).

But what role do interest groups play after an initial burst of external liberalization, and in postcrisis conditions when "normal" politics returns? Here the picture differs across countries and regions. In some parts of the world, protectionist coalitions have halted or slowed down liberalization. This is the case with "nomenklatura" coalitions in Russia, Ukraine, and other parts of the ex–Soviet Union. Elsewhere, radical opening has triggered major economic shifts in favor of sectors exposed to the world economy. Traditional protectionist interests have been weakened, and countervailing coalitions have emerged. The latter comprise exporters, users of imported inputs, multinationals with global production networks, and cities and regions seeking to be magnets for trade and FDI. These interests lobby for the maintenance and extension of open trade and FDI regimes.[12] This has happened in strong-liberalizing countries in east Asia, eastern Europe, and Latin America. It happened in Australia and New Zealand from the early 1980s. It is also evident in India after the 1991 reforms.

Ideas

> *It is the word in season that does much to decide the result.*
>
> —John Stuart Mill

> *Madmen who hear voices in the air are distilling their frenzy from the academic scribblings of some defunct economist or political philosopher. Indeed the world is ruled by little else.*
>
> —John Maynard Keynes

It is always difficult to gauge the influence of ideas (or ideology) in policy.[13] But practical observation teaches us that the prevailing climate of ideas, interacting with interests and events, can entrench or sway this or that set of policies. A policy consensus on import substitution, state planning, and foreign aid was strongly embedded in developing-country governments and international organizations up to the 1970s. This was buttressed by a postcolonial political ideology of mercantilist state-building, and an interventionist consensus in development economics.[14] This set of ideas was overturned by what came to be called the Washington Consensus, which reflected sea changes in political ideology and in development economics. The latter returned to classical and neoclassical foundations, emphasizing market-based pricing, "outward orientation," and the prevalence of "government failure" over "market failure," not to mention a dose of aid skepticism.

Washington Consensus ideas took stronger hold in countries where reforms were substantial, especially in ministries of finance, central banks, and presidential and prime ministerial offices. These agencies tend to be the cockpits of policy reform. But now the climate of ideas has changed somewhat. This does not presage a return to full-blown pre–Washington Consensus thinking. The pendulum, however, is swinging toward more attention to market failure and government intervention, for example, to ease back on further liberalization, expand "policy space" and promote infant industries, defend "food security," and increase foreign aid. The question is what effect this is having, and is likely to have, on trade policies.

Institutions

In the broad sense, institutions are the steel frame of the economy, its "formal rules and informal constraints," according to Douglas North. The legal framework governing property rights and contracts, and production and consumption, comes to mind. "Formal rules" comprise bankruptcy laws, competition laws, regulations governing financial markets and corporate governance, and much else besides. "Informal constraints" are (often nonlegal) traditions and norms influencing the intersecting worlds of business, government, and the law.

Evidently, "institutions" are much broader and more difficult to pin down than "policies," and the two are of course intimately connected. Historically conditioned institutions, domestic and external, set the scene for government action, interest-group lobbying, and the influence of ideas. They are the arena for policy choices and their implementation. Generalizing about institutional constraints on policy choice, and how this might explain differences in national and regional economic performance over time, is notoriously difficult. To what extent must "good" institutions be in place before "good" policies can take hold and work their magic? Conversely, to what extent are institutions the result, rather than the cause, of policy choices? These are chicken-and-egg questions.

In the narrow sense, institutions are the organizational map of decisionmaking at the junction where politics and public policy meet business and society. On trade policy, this map is much more complicated than it used to be. Trade policy is no longer just about a clutch of border instruments and the preserve of trade ministries. It is increasingly "trade related," a matter of nonborder regulation reaching deep into the domestic economy and its institutions. That is reflected in more complex multilateral, regional, and bilateral trade agreements. This brings in agencies across the range of government, and many actors outside government as well. Now the management of trade policy involves the division of labor among the executive, legislature, and judiciary; the role of the lead ministry; the participation of other ministries and regulatory agencies on trade and trade-related policies; the WTO mission in Geneva; interagency coordination within government; the involvement of nongovernmental actors, such as business and unions, and now including nongovernmental organizations and think tanks; and the role of donors and international organizations.

Inasmuch as one can make generalizations about institutions and trade policy in developing countries, here are a couple. First, it is the more advanced developing countries (with regard to per capita income and human welfare indicators) that have liberalized more and plugged themselves better into globalization than other developing countries. They have lower trade and FDI barriers, higher ratios of trade and FDI to gross domestic product, and better-performing tradable sectors of the economy. They also have stronger institutions in the broad sense: better enforcement of property rights and contracts (i.e., the rule of law), better-functioning judiciaries and public administration, better-regulated financial markets, a stronger competition culture, less corruption, and so on. This is the divide that separates Chile and a few other Latin American countries, eastern Europe, the northeast Asian and southeast Asian Tigers, and a tiny handful of African countries (Mauritius, Botswana, and South Africa) from the rest. There are, however, two gigantic anomalies: China and India. Both are still low-income countries with weak institutions (going by some of the indicators mentioned earlier). Institutional improvements have taken place, but these have lagged well behind big policy shifts—not least lower trade and FDI restrictions—and fast-paced global integration.[15]

Second, looking at institutions in the narrower organizational sense, strong and sustained trade-policy and wider economic-policy reforms were driven, more often than not, by powerful presidential or prime ministerial offices, ministries of finance, and central banks, insulated from blocking pressures in other parts of government and outside government. This was more pronounced in advanced developing countries than elsewhere. These countries also have stronger capacity, with regard to qualified, experienced manpower and other resources, for formulating and implementing trade policy, whether done unilaterally or through international negotiations and agreements. Again, China and India are exceptional: they are low-income countries with relatively weak institutions (in the broad sense), but with relatively strong trade-policy capacity.

Factor Endowments

Explaining the trajectory of policy reforms is not complete without factoring in the relative mix of land (or natural resources), labor, and capital in an economy.[16] We know from recent economic history that the star developing-country performers are from east Asia. These countries had different starting positions, but, at a certain stage of development, relative labor abundance allowed them to break into labor-intensive manufactured exports, which became an engine of growth and in turn aided poverty reduction and human welfare improvement. Of course, this was not inevitable: it depended on the right policies and improving institutions. South Asia, with similar factor endowments, remained stuck on a low-growth, high-poverty path because it did not adopt market-based policies.

Latin American and African countries, on the other hand, are largely land or resource abundant and labor scarce. Absent import substitution policies, they are better able to exploit comparative advantage in land and resources—as Brazil, Argentina, Chile, Australia, and New Zealand have done in agriculture since they liberalized, and as all the latter and many other countries besides are doing in the present China-driven commodities boom.

Thus, a simple story based on early 21st-century comparative advantage would point to all-around gains from trade for technologically advanced and capital-abundant countries in the West, the labor-abundant countries of east and south Asia, and land- and resource-abundant countries elsewhere.

But the political economy of factor endowments reveals a different and more problematic story. Arguably, land- and resource-abundant countries are at a structural disadvantage compared with labor-abundant countries. By plugging into global markets for manufacturing, and now labor-intensive services too, the latter seem to be on sustainable growth paths. Labor-intensive exports attract FDI (and the technology and skills that come with it) and feed quickly into poverty-reducing, welfare-improving employment and, more gradually, into better infrastructure and institutions. This creates and strengthens a constellation of interests to support open trade and FDI policies.

However, given their relatively high price of labor, land- and resource-abundant countries seem to be crowded out of global manufacturing markets by east Asian (especially Chinese) competition.[17] This leaves them dependent on cyclical and volatile commodities markets. FDI in resource-abundant countries tends to be capital intensive and to generate big rents in not-so-competitive market segments. Often, the result is an FDI enclave, without an employment, technology, or wealth spillover to the rest of the economy, but with big profits to distribute among a corrupt local business and political elite. Most countries dependent on resources have the interest-group constellation to squander rents from resource booms, but not to spread wealth and improve governance and institutions. A retreat to protectionism, however, would repeat past mistakes and make matters worse. This is the dilemma inherent in the present "China-in-Africa" phenomenon. But there are notable exceptions to the "resource-curse" rule: Chile has successfully exploited a comparative advantage in agriculture and resources (mainly copper) through liberal trade policies, while diversifying the economic base and improving institutions. That is also true of Australia and New Zealand.

Preliminary Summary

In most strong-liberalizing countries, a political or macroeconomic crisis has led to a big opening of the economy; new open-economy interest-group constellations have emerged to counter traditional protectionist interests; open-market ideas have become entrenched; and stronger institutions are better able to support and manage open-market policies. Some countries, for example, China and others in east Asia, have gone down this path without the catalyst of a macroeconomic crisis. Generally, advanced developing countries have more liberal trade policies and stronger institutions and are more globally integrated than the rest. China and India are the two big exceptions: they have liberalized extensively and integrated fast into the global economy, but with still-weak institutions. Labor-abundant countries in east Asia, and now in south Asia, best fit the big picture of external liberalization and global integration. The picture looks different in countries that have liberalized less and globalized less. Resource-abundant countries in Latin America, Africa, the Middle East, Russia, and other parts of the ex–Soviet Union are now doing well in the China-driven commodities boom. But their political economy is problematic: their predatory governments and interest groups are geared more to squandering rents than to creating and spreading wealth sustainably.

Multitrack Trade Policy

Another way of cutting into trade-policy reform is to look at it on several tracks. Some reforms are carried out *unilaterally*; others *reciprocally* through (bilateral, regional, or multilateral) trade negotiations, or in agreements with donors. Most developing countries now do trade policy on all these tracks concurrently, though the relative balance differs from country to country.

What follows is a brief summary of the main features of "multitrack" trade policy in developing countries. Chapters 4, 5, and 6 will flesh out the detail on the WTO, preferential trade agreements, and unilateral liberalization, especially in Asia. Foreign aid has also been an important factor in trade-policy reforms—in some countries more than in others. That is also examined in this section.

Unilateral Liberalization

This is the Nike strategy ("Just Do It."). Governments "liberalize first and negotiate later," as Mart Laar, the former prime minister of Estonia, puts it. In theory, this makes good economic sense. The gain from liberalization comes from imports, which release domestic resources for more productive uses, including exports, and help open the door to inward investment.[18] Why, therefore, delay the gain by waiting for cumbersome, bureaucratic trade negotiations to deliver the goods? Unilateral liberalization can make political sense too, as it can be tailored to local conditions rather than being dictated by "one-size-fits-all" donor conditionality and international trade agreements.

The British led the way with unilateral free trade in the 19th century. The first half of the 20th century witnessed unilateral protectionism by country after country. Since 1945, most developed countries have liberalized reciprocally, through the General Agreement on Tariffs and Trade and bilateral and regional trade agreements.

But most developing-country trade and FDI liberalization has been done unilaterally, not through trade negotiations. The World Bank estimates that two-thirds of developing-country tariff liberalization since the early 1980s has been done unilaterally.[19] The strongest liberalizers have been unilateral liberalizers: the east Asian countries, now led by China; Chile and Mexico; the east European countries; and Australia and New Zealand. Nearly all of India's post-1991 liberalization has been done unilaterally.

Multilateral Liberalization

The rationale for liberalization through "multilateral reciprocity" is that unilateral liberalization is politically difficult under 20th- and 21st-century conditions of democratic politics and strong interest-group activity. General Agreement on Trade and Tariffs (GATT) and WTO negotiations have helped to contain protectionist interests and mobilize exporting interests, and multilateral agreements provide fair, nondiscriminatory rules for all.

Multilateral liberalization was successful during the GATT when the latter had a relatively slim-line agenda, clublike decisionmaking dominated by a handful of developed countries (especially the United States and EU), and the glue of cold war alliance politics. It has proved spectacularly unsuccessful in the WTO, given the organization's large, unwieldy agenda; the chaotic United Nations style of decisionmaking in a vastly expanded membership; and the lack of military alliances after the cold war. Deadlock in the Doha round probably shows that future multilateral liberalization will be elusive, and modest at best. Arguably, the best the WTO can hope for is to lock in preexisting unilateral liberalization through binding commitments, and gradually improve the functioning of nondiscriminatory multilateral rules. Even that will be a tall order, given the parlous state of the WTO. There is every prospect that multilateral trade rules will be undermined by major players seeking to evade them, with extra pressure coming from proliferating, discriminatory bilateral and regional trade agreements. Weaker multilateral rules will be a much bigger cost for developing countries than the extra multilateral liberalization forgone as a result of Doha round failure.

Bilateral and Regional Liberalization

Proponents argue that small clubs of like-minded members can take liberalization and rules faster, wider, and deeper than in the

WTO, and act as "building blocks" to further multilateral liberalization and rule making. Skeptics say they are "stumbling blocks,"
diverting attention from the WTO, creating "spaghetti bowls" of
discriminatory trade restrictions, and generally favoring powerful
players at the expense of the weak.

The reality is mixed. Nondiscriminatory unilateral and multilateral liberalization blunt the damaging effects of discriminatory trade
agreements. There is little prospect of the world economy retreating
to the warring trade blocs of the 1930s. Strong, "WTO-plus" free trade
agreements (FTAs) can also make sense in certain circumstances. But
the record in developing-country regions is not encouraging. Latin
America and Africa have a messy patchwork of weak FTAs that do
not liberalize much trade or improve on WTO rules, but do create
complications, especially through trade-restricting rules of origin,
and divert attention both from the WTO and from unilateral reforms.
This is also the emerging picture of FTAs in east and south Asia.

The Role of Donors[20]

Foreign aid, with conditions attached by the IMF, World Bank, and
other donors, has clearly played a big part in driving Washington
Consensus–type reforms in many developing countries. This has
gone way beyond developing countries' (relatively weak) liberalizing commitments in the WTO and FTAs. Arguably, unilateral liberalization has not been truly "unilateral" when it has depended on
donor policy preferences and aid with strings attached. The record
of IMF stabilization packages and World Bank structural adjustment
packages has been mixed at best, and certainly disappointing compared with optimistic expectations in the 1980s.[21] Often, donor-
driven reforms have proceeded in stops and starts, with reversals
en route. Projected growth and poverty-alleviation effects have not
materialized. The politics of aid is even more dubious than its economics. "Conditionality" is empty rhetoric when self-serving interests at both ends of the pipeline ensure that aid continues to flow,
even when promised reforms are not delivered. And the perception
that Western donors are imposing reforms on otherwise reluctant
countries is hardly sustainable: local "ownership" is lacking (to borrow aid jargon), and it invites a backlash and reform reversal at
home.[22]

The bottom line is that countries that have seen strong, sustained,
unilateral liberalizing reforms are those whose governments have

driven reforms ("from below," as it were) rather than having them imposed by donors ("from above"). Aid at its best has smoothed short-term adjustments, and donor conditionality has provided a *"Good Housekeeping* Seal of Approval"—an international signal of reform credibility—more than anything else. In these countries (most in east Asia and eastern Europe, and a few in Latin America), aid has not been central to reform success. Where there has been more reliance on aid and donor conditionality, reforms have a far worse record. This applies to Africa in particular.

Seen in this light, the new conventional wisdom on aid is wrong-headed and dangerous. The United Nations Millennium Project and the Africa Commission report both propose to double or even triple aid between 2005 and 2015, particularly with Africa in mind. The United Nations idea—or rather, Jeffrey Sachs's idea—is a new version of the old principle of aid: poor countries lack resources to invest, and donors have to fill this "financing gap" with a "big push" of investment if growth is ever to occur.[23] A sudden and massive increase of aid threatens to repeat past mistakes and provide extra incentives to delay and derail, not promote, market-based reforms. Available evidence shows that aid does not improve the productivity of investment; it diverts funds to stimulate government consumption and current spending; it has a negative effect on domestic savings; and, by expanding the role of already-dysfunctional governments, it breeds waste and corruption. In short, this approach is misguided top-down intervention.[24]

A softer version of aid optimism, associated with the World Bank, assumes that countries are poor because of bad policy choices and weak institutions and that aid can lock in already-accomplished reforms and facilitate additional reforms.[25] This view is politically naive, though a convenient fiction for elites who profit from the aid business. The main objection is that aid has not, and probably will not, be a good midwife to market-based reforms. On the contrary, aid is given more often than not to support failed policies, and there is a high incidence of repeat lending to governments without a good track record of market-based reforms.

A particular version of the aid-to-reform idea is the "aid-for-trade" scheme that is now discussed in the Doha round. No one has yet defined its modus operandi. Is it a structural adjustment program, an unemployment insurance program, a budget support program, an industrial promotion program, or something else? Whatever the purpose, the history of aid warns us of the perils of such a scheme. A basic problem with the idea is that countries should be protected from the market-based structural adjustment that trade liberalization entails. That is in direct conflict with the reality of development.

Preliminary Summary

Strong reforming countries have relied overwhelmingly on unilateral liberalization. This has sometimes translated into stronger multilateral commitments and more flexible, pragmatic participation in the WTO. China and Vietnam are the textbook examples. But further substantial liberalization through trade negotiations, whether in the WTO or FTAs, is unlikely. Finally, aid-induced liberalization has not really worked: its political economy is highly dubious. Hence, it is a mistake to rely even more on aid for further market-based reforms.

What Lessons for Future Liberalization?

To recapitulate, the conditions for further liberalization and associated structural reforms are more difficult today than they were in the heyday of the Washington Consensus. Reform complacency results from a postcrisis environment of buoyant growth and normal interest-group politics. There is dissatisfaction with previous reforms in parts of the developing world. Some anti-liberalization ideas are enjoying a minor revival. Finally, the politics of "second-generation" trade-policy reforms is proving much more difficult than that of "first-generation" reforms. The latter involve the reduction and removal of border barriers. This is relatively simple technically and can be done quickly—though politically these measures are rarely easy. The former are all about complex domestic (though trade-related) regulation, such as services regulation, regulation of food-safety and technical standards, intellectual property protection, public procurement, customs administration, and competition rules. These reforms are technically and administratively difficult and take time to implement. They demand a minimum of capacity across government, especially for implementation and enforcement. Above all, they are politically very sensitive, as they affect entrenched interests that are extremely difficult to dislodge.

Still, there is a strong case for further market-based reforms in general, and for external liberalization in particular. Reduction of what are still high barriers to trade, foreign investment, and the cross-border movement of people holds out the promise of higher growth, significant poverty reduction, and improvements in human welfare. Stalled reforms and reform reversal threaten to deprive hundreds of millions of people of the life chances they deserve. These are the stakes. Against this backdrop, the following challenges lie ahead:

"First-division" Reformers

These are the 20–25 developing countries—the "new globalizers"—that have already gone far with macroeconomic stabilization and internal and external liberalization. They have plugged themselves into globalization. Their task is to go further with dismantling border barriers to trade and opening the door to FDI. But their bigger challenge is to make much more progress on trade-related domestic reforms—the "structural" and "institutional" reforms where progress to date has been too slow. This entails tackling the second-generation issues mentioned above. What is needed is a culture of permanent, incremental reforms, mainly of the second-generation variety, that build on the foundations of first-generation reforms, so that the economy adapts flexibly to changing global conditions. That is easier said than done. The great difficulty lies in doing serious reforms in conditions of normal interest-group politics, without an economic crisis to concentrate minds. But the alternative is creeping sclerosis in times of plenty and excessive reliance on a crisis for the next reform wave.[26] That cannot be good for long-term political, social, and economic health.

Such are the broad trade-policy priorities for first-division developing countries. In this context, the following points deserve emphasis.

First, there needs to be a clearer link between trade policy, on the one hand, and *domestic* economic-policy and institutional reforms, on the other hand. Trade policy should be coupled strongly with competition-friendly measures to improve the domestic business climate. It should be better hitched to domestic reforms. For example, there should be ways of linking trade and FDI liberalization, and trade-related regulatory reform, to measures to shorten and simplify regulations that hinder business at home. Such red tape includes procedural hurdles to overcome before starting a business: dealing with various licensing procedures, registering property, getting access to credit, employing workers, paying taxes, and protecting investors and bankruptcy procedures. Red tape directly affecting exports and imports includes the documentation, time taken, and costs of clearing goods through customs. These regulations are documented, classified, and ranked in the World Bank's annual *Doing Business* report. Second-generation trade-policy reforms also depend on the quality of public administration and the rule of law (i.e., the quality of the legal framework governing property rights and contracts, and their enforcement by the judicial system). These relate to some of the World Bank's governance indicators and cross-country rankings.[27]

Second, and following directly from the previous point, trade policy should be seen less through the prism of trade negotiations and international organizations and (as argued earlier) more through the prism of the domestic economy. Second-generation reforms in particular are bundled up with domestic politics and economics; initiating and implementing them is overwhelmingly a domestic affair; and the scope for productive international negotiations and solutions is restricted. That is already becoming evident with the regulation of services trade and trade-related product standards, and of policies toward inward investment. It will become even more evident as global production networks and the movement of people across borders bite ever deeper into domestic institutions.

As trade policy becomes ever more entwined with domestic policies and institutions, it follows that there should be more reliance on unilateral measures, including external liberalization, and correspondingly less reliance on reciprocal liberalization through the WTO and preferential trade agreements. Unilateral reforms should then be locked in through stronger WTO commitments. This should be the foundation for advancing national market-access and rule-making interests in the WTO. Governments should also exercise caution with PTAs, avoiding quick and dirty ones and engaging only in those that are comprehensive, WTO-plus, and clearly linked to competition-enhancing domestic reforms.

Third, there should be much more policy *transparency*. Trade policy decisionmaking is usually opaque. Too little is known and understood about the effects of this or that set of trade policies. Consequently, public discussion of policy choices is usually uninformed and misguided. One should add that this applies almost as much to developed countries as to developing countries. For example, anti-dumping and rules-of-origin procedures in the EU are shrouded in secretive, discretionary, and ultimately arbitrary behavior, with restricted external access to information. The situation is not much better elsewhere.

What is lacking is what Patrick Messerlin calls a "culture of evaluation."[28] Independent think tanks and even government bodies should do much more detailed research and analysis on the costs and benefits of trade policies in different sectors of the economy, and then disseminate findings to the public. This would facilitate more informed, intelligent public discussion of policy choices.[29] One model to examine is that of the Australian Productivity Commission (formerly the Tariff Board). This is a government body, but it is independent and has statutory powers. It provides research and analysis on trade-related issues in Australia, and its conclusions do make their way into the public debate. The Tariff Board's groundbreaking work did much to reveal the costs of protection to the Australian public back in the 1970s, at a time when Australia was a highly protected economy. This generated much public discussion at the time, and in many ways prepared the ground for the radical opening of the Australian economy in the 1980s. Such "transparency boards" could be set up at relatively low cost in developing countries.

Taken together, these reform priorities are as much about *simplicity* and *transparency* as they are about *liberalization*. The case for transparency has been made above. Simplicity is all about making complex bureaucratic procedures shorter, more predictable, and also more transparent. This would lessen the costs of doing business—for domestic *and* foreign traders and investors. Hence the importance of linking trade policy to nitty-gritty domestic reforms.

Fundamentally, these reforms boil down to restructuring the state, away from the large overactive state that intervenes badly across the range of economic activity and toward the limited state that performs a smaller number of core functions well. The latter should focus on providing and enforcing a framework of rules for market-based competition. To return to Michael Oakeshott's distinction, the state should be an "umpire" of a "civic association," not an "estate manager" of an "enterprise association."

"Lower-division" Reformers

These countries, overwhelmingly in the low-income and least-developed bracket, have higher border barriers than first-division reformers, in addition to bigger domestic obstacles to trade and investment. They are less globalized. Their first priority should be to reduce border barriers and simple nonborder barriers (such as some red tape procedures that give them low rankings in the World Bank's *Doing Business* report). They have less capacity than first-division reformers for implementing more complex second-generation reforms. These could wait until the easier reforms are done. The real dilemma is that countries at the bottom of this pile, especially among the least-developed countries, are mired in political instability and civil strife, with failed and failing states that do not perform the most basic public functions. Such countries do not have the capacity to implement even simple reforms. Aid-driven solutions have failed, but what is the substitute?

All countries face reform complacency and fatigue. But labor-abundant countries that have inserted themselves into global production networks are most likely to have interest-group coalitions and institutions to defend existing open-market reforms and promote further reforms. Resource-abundant countries have a weaker political-economy base. They are more likely to let reforms lapse and squander the rents from commodity booms. They are doubly challenged in building coalitions of interests to keep reforms going and to strengthen institutions so that wealth is both generated sustainably and spread widely.

Several other policy challenges come to mind, all directly or indirectly related to trade policy. Here is a brief list, with equally brief answers.

1. How should trade-policy reforms be sequenced with other reforms, such as those relating to macroeconomic policy? Should reforms be fast or gradual?

There are no general answers to these questions. They depend on circumstances, and expediency will dictate different answers in different places at different times. What matters more is the general thrust: a medium- to long-term commitment to liberalize in the direction of a market-based, globally integrated economy.

2. What is the link with political systems? Is democracy or authoritarianism better suited to market-based policy reform? Do such reforms have a better chance under right-wing or left-wing governments?

Again, there are no general answers. For every example to support one thesis, there is a counterexample to support the opposite thesis. Reforms have succeeded in widely differing political systems, and under governments of different political hues, just as they have failed across the spectrum of political systems and partisan politics.

3. What role is there for industrial policy?

There is leeway for experimentation, adapted to different local conditions. Economywide measures, such as improving transport and communications infrastructure, as well as education and skills, can dovetail with trade and wider economic-policy reforms. So can other "soft" measures, such as trade and investment promotion through information dissemination, organizing of trade fairs, and the like. But selective promotion and protection of this or that industry has a questionable record, and "hard" industrial policy of the picking-winners variety has an abysmal record. It should be avoided.

4. What about social policies?

Are social safety nets needed alongside liberalizing reforms? How generous should they be? Should "losers" be compensated? These questions of distribution and equity elicit quite different responses. The classical-liberal response is to keep government limited, focused on its role to provide and enforce a framework of rules for an open, competitive market economy. Basic social safety nets should be provided where affordable. Beyond that, the classical liberal has little interest in redistribution. In contrast, the social democratic response is to give high priority to redistribution, with government playing an active role.

These debates have taken place mostly in developed countries, but they are of course relevant to developing countries. On the one hand, developing countries have less financial scope for redistribution compared with developed countries. They also have bigger institutional constraints. Ambitious social policies risk scattering scarce resources that should be focused on liberalizing reforms. On the other hand, big and widening differences between income groups and regions could undermine popular acceptance of core reforms.

Here also there are no easy, general blueprints. There is room for experimentation and trial-and-error learning. But one thing is needed: better delivery of existing public services, including the provision of social safety nets. These are the last bastions of the command economy. Administrative mechanisms squander public funds and fail to serve those most in need. More market mechanisms are needed, including competition from private-sector suppliers of services. That also opens up possibilities for trade, FDI, and cross-border labor movement in traditional public services such as health care, education, and the utilities, and even beyond to cover housing, social security, and pensions. These "third-generation" reforms are the next frontier.

Conclusion

The naysayers, from the hard and soft Left, and the conservative Right, hold that liberalization has not delivered the goods. They argue for various forms of government intervention, at national and international levels, to tame "market fundamentalism" and "neoliberal globalization." Interventionist ideas on trade (and aid) are not new; they hark back to pre–Adam Smith, "preanalytic" mercantilism (as Schumpeter called it). What they have in common is an age-old distrust of markets and faith in government intervention—what David Henderson calls "New Millennium Collectivism."[30] Such collectivist thinking is on the rise again. But it is still wrong and dangerous. It glosses over the damage done by interventionist policies in the past and misreads the recent and historical evidence. The latter shows that external liberalization, as part of broad market-based reforms, has worked: countries that have become more open to the world economy have grown faster and become richer than those that have opened up less or remained closed.

There is much unfinished business. Barriers to trade, and the cross-border movement of capital and people, remain high, indeed more so in developing countries than in developed countries. But a combination of material circumstances and changes in the climate of ideas makes market-based reforms more difficult now than was the case a decade ago. The stakes, however, are too important for reform challenges to be avoided. Although there is no imminent threat of global economic collapse, stalled reforms threaten to slow down globalization's advance, thereby depriving the world's least advantaged people of the life chances that globalization offers. That would reinforce strong pressures, from an alliance of old-style protectionist interests and new-style ideological forces, for overactive government to restrict economic freedom and the operation of the market economy. That is why new-old collectivist ideas need to be countered with full force.

Thus, it falls to free trade's friends to make a strong case for further reforms, including external liberalization, and practically go about assembling reform coalitions. To borrow J. S. Mill's felicitous phrase again, they should spread their word *in season with* global political currents, anti-protectionist producer and consumer interests, and (often unanticipated) events.

4. The World Trade Organization

The great political virtue of multilateralism, far exceeding in importance its economic virtues, is that it makes it economically possible for most countries, even if small, poor and weak, to live in freedom and with chances of prosperity without having to come to special terms with some Great Power.

—Jacob Viner

In recent years, the impression has often been given of a vehicle with a proliferation of backseat drivers, each seeking a different destination, with no map and no intention of asking the way.

—The Sutherland Report

The quotes above signify the highs and lows of the World Trade Organization. Its establishment in 1995 was hailed as a significant strengthening of multilateral trade rules. This was supposed to transform a "power-based" trading system into a "rules-based" one, protecting the small and vulnerable from the predation of the big and powerful. It gave flesh, blood, and, above all, legal expression to the founding spirit of the General Agreement on Tariffs and Trade that Jacob Viner wrote about a half century earlier. Prevailing winds outside Geneva were also blowing favorably: liberalization was in the air almost everywhere, in the Organisation for Economic Co-operation and Development, the developing world, and in the ex–command economies.

A little more than a decade later, the Doha round seems to be perpetually stalemated and on the verge of collapse. It listed heavily from the start, and several attempts to right it have failed. As the Sutherland Report indicates, the WTO seems immovable: it is full of cacophonous navigators without a compass, steering wildly in all sorts of vague and contradictory directions. Outside Geneva, the winds of liberalization have subsided, there are countercurrents buffeting market-based reforms, and governments seem keener to negotiate a hotchpotch of preferential trade agreements (PTAs) than to do serious business in the WTO.

How has this come to pass? And what is the future of the WTO after the Doha round? Is it capable of upholding multilateral rules for open international trade? Can it help secure and extend the global market economy? Or is it a lost cause, crippled by anti-market forces within and without?

From GATT to WTO

The trade economist's textbook argument is that unilateral liberalization is the "first-best" method to open the national economy to external competition. But, given the realities of modern politics—interest-group lobbying for protection, ingrained mercantilist thinking, and the perception that liberalization hurts the poor and vulnerable—this is difficult to achieve in practice—hence, the merit of the "multilateralized reciprocity" that the GATT/WTO embodies. The following advantages come to mind:

- Intergovernment negotiations and binding international obligations help protect governments against powerful protectionist interests at home and mobilize the support of domestic exporters.
- WTO rules provide rights to market access for exports and rights against the arbitrary protection and predation of more powerful players. This is particularly important for developing countries.
- Multilateral rules can bolster domestic reforms and reinforce their credibility with exporters, importers, local and foreign investors, and, not least, consumers. This is another way of saying that the WTO, at its best, is a helpful auxiliary to good national governance.

This standard raison d'être was easier said in the old GATT than done in the WTO. In many ways, the WTO is the victim of its own success—the successful conclusion of the Uruguay round and the huge transition from the GATT to the WTO. Six underlying trends need to be highlighted, all of which ring alarm bells:

1. The Uruguay round agreements not only take the WTO wider, with broader sectoral coverage, but they also go much deeper into domestic regulation than previous GATT agreements.

Understandably so: if the WTO disregarded domestic regulatory barriers, lower protection at the border would be nullified by higher protection behind it—hence the need for procedural disciplines on regulations on services, subsidies, food-safety and technical standards, customs valuation, and much else that is "trade related."

However, a common minimum-standards approach to domestic regulation can lead to regulatory overload. The biggest danger is a creeping *standards harmonization* agenda. Detailed, prescriptive regulations are intended (at least implicitly) to bring developing-country standards up to developed-country norms. The Trade-Related Aspects of Intellectual Property Rights agreement—the most regulation-heavy of all Uruguay round agreements—sets the precedent for pressure to harmonize labor, environmental, food-safety, and other product standards. This "intrusionism" in the domestic policies and institutions of the developing world is noxious: economically, it can raise developing countries' costs out of line with comparative advantages and has a chilling effect on labor-intensive exports; and politically, it goes too far in curtailing national regulatory autonomy.[1]

2. The GATT *reciprocity* model effectively tackled border barriers that are relatively easy to quantify, compare, and bargain over. Trade policy today, in contrast, encompasses complex, opaque domestic regulations on all manner of trade-related issues for which data are lacking and comparison is more subjective. These "second-generation" issues are intimately bound up with local institutional particularities, administratively demanding and politically very sensitive. They are less amenable to reciprocal bargaining and one-size-fits-all international rules than is the case with relatively simple tariffs and quotas. That makes progress in the WTO elusive.

3. The *legalization* of the WTO is double-edged. Dispute settlement is much stronger than it was in the GATT: it has acquired legal teeth and bite. And it has worked rather well: increasing numbers of developed and developing countries have used it, and compliance has generally been good. However, given its quasi-automaticity, governments have more incentive to fill

Figure 4.1
WTO MEMBER COUNTRIES THAT SIGNED THE GATT, 1985–2007

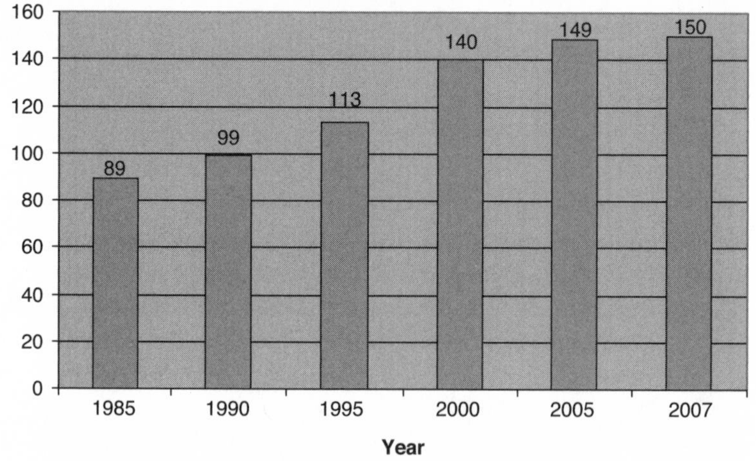

SOURCE: "Understanding the WTO: The Organization," WTO, Geneva, 2007, www.wto.org/english/thewto_e/whatis_e/tif_e/org6_e.htm; "The 128 Countries That Had Signed GATT by 1994," WTO, Geneva, www.wto.org/english/thewto_e/gattmem_e.htm.

NOTE: Countries having signed GATT 1985–1990 and countries having entered the WTO 1995–2007.

in regulatory gaps in ambiguously worded WTO agreements through litigation—especially when diplomacy and negotiations are not working. This is a dangerous and slippery slope. A large, diverse gathering of sovereign nations such as the WTO, with, at best, a brittle political consensus, must make collective policy choices through diplomacy and negotiation, not by default through dispute settlement. The Dispute Settlement Body simply does not enjoy the political consensus or legitimacy to "create" law as a means of driving policy.[2]

4. The WTO is increasingly *politicized*. Externally, it faces the brunt of the anti-globalization backlash and is rocked by a combination of old-style protectionist interests and new-style nongovernmental organizations (NGOs). Even more vexing are its deeper internal fissures. The vast expansion of membership since the late 1980s (see Figure 4.1) has added new sets of

developing-country interests and preferences, and it has made decisionmaking more unwieldy and snaillike. Day by day, the "UN-ization" of the WTO has gathered pace. Windy rhetoric, adversarial point scoring, political grandstanding, and procedural nitpicking seem to have substituted for serious decisionmaking. The GATT escaped these pitfalls because it had a reasonably clear purpose, a relatively slim-line negotiating agenda, and intimate, clublike decisionmaking among a handful of key players. The WTO, sadly, has degenerated into a talking shop reminiscent of the United Nations General Assembly.

5. The *bilateralization* and *regionalization* of the world economy, that is, the accelerating spread of discriminatory bilateral and regional trade agreements, seems to be preprogrammed, not least in reaction to stalled multilateral liberalization. PTAs are not uniformly bad, but they do lead to a "spaghetti bowl" of discrimination and red tape in international trade, driven by power politics. This is precisely what GATT-style multilateralism was supposed to contain and reduce. PTAs also risk diverting political attention and negotiating resources away from the WTO. More on this in the following chapter.

6. The "high politics" of *foreign policy* matters for the "low politics" of trade policy. The GATT was founded in the early stages of the cold war, and the Western alliance held it together during the cold war. That glue has since dissolved. In particular, the United States and Western Europe lack the strategic bonds of a shared security policy to bridge differences and forge common positions in trade negotiations.

Taken together, these pressures have virtually crippled the old GATT's traditional strength: its ability to deliver results through effective diplomacy and negotiation. A wider and more intrusive regulatory agenda makes it more difficult to maintain political legitimacy with governments and interest groups (now including NGOs). It has also blurred the WTO's focus and made the organization drift toward multiple and contradictory objectives. It has become painfully difficult to make the GATT reciprocity model work with the plethora of nonborder issues on the WTO's agenda. Stalled negotiations increase the temptation to settle sensitive policy dilemmas through adversarial litigation, which further tests the political legitimacy of the system. The hyperinflation of membership, with the

61

attendant desire to widen the decisionmaking circle and make it more inclusive and participatory, strains the workability of the system to its limits. And last, the unifying glue of the cold war has dissolved. For these reasons, the WTO as a *negotiating* mechanism has not really functioned since the late 1990s.

The Doha Round

WTO members tried to launch a new "Millennium round" of trade negotiations, but failed spectacularly at the disastrous Seattle Ministerial Conference in late 1999. A new round was launched at the Doha Ministerial Conference in November 2001—but only due to September 11, and the subsequent perception of global political and economic crisis. Hence, the "Doha Development Agenda"—the official title of the round—merits the sobriquet "the Bin Laden round."

WTO members agreed to a large, complex, and ambitious agenda, with 21 subjects dealt with in eight negotiating groups. There was a market-access core, that is, negotiations on further trade liberalization, as demanded by the United States, the Cairns Group (of leading developed and developing-country agricultural exporters), and a few others. Developing countries demanded the inclusion of the "implementation agenda" (flexibility and assistance in implementing Uruguay round agreements), flexibility in interpreting WTO rules on patent protection, and, more generically, a reconsideration of special and differential treatment (more favorable treatment for developing countries under WTO agreements). The European Union managed to get trade-and-environment and the "Singapore issues" (competition, investment, trade facilitation, and transparency in government procurement) included. And there were to be new negotiations on WTO rules (anti-dumping, fisheries subsidies, regional trade agreements, and dispute settlement).[3]

Very little progress was made from the start. Ministers were supposed to put a negotiating framework together for the second half of the round at the Fifth Ministerial Conference, held in Cancún in September 2003. This collapsed in all-around acrimony, chaos, and farce. Only in July 2004 was such a framework put together. This whittled down a previously large and unwieldy agenda into one focused on the key market-access issues (agriculture, services, and nonagricultural goods). Trade facilitation was also included, while the other three Singapore issues were deleted. After that, negotiations became deadlocked again.

The following Ministerial Conference, in Hong Kong in December 2005, delivered a pathetic runt of a package: agreement was reached on relatively minor issues (eventual abolition of EU agricultural export subsidies; Intellectual Property–related decisions concerning developing countries; extension of duty-free and quota-free access to least-developing countries' exports; and "aid for trade"), whereas all major policy decisions concerning market access were postponed.[4] There was little narrowing of differences in subsequent months, and the round was "suspended indefinitely" in late July 2006. By then, there was no real chance of concluding an agreement before the supposedly final deadline: the expiry of U.S. Trade Promotion Authority (which the president needs in order to negotiate and conclude trade agreements) in July 2007. Negotiations formally restarted in February 2007. At the time of writing, they show little sign of breaking the logjam.

What should be achieved? There is still much to do on market access. Direct border barriers to trade remain high in both developed countries and developing countries. Although the EU and the United States have low average tariffs, they retain high to very high tariffs in agriculture, textiles and clothing, and other labor-intensive goods—the sectors of major export potential for developing countries. Huge agricultural subsidies in the OECD continue to distort trade. Widespread anti-dumping actions and unreasonably onerous food-safety, technical, and other standards also have a chilling effect on developing-country exports. Not least, developing countries have noticeably higher tariffs and nontariff barriers than developed countries, whose main effect is to severely restrict imports from other developing countries. (On market-access barriers, see Tables 3.1 and 3.2 and Figures 3.1–3.5 in Chapter 3.)

Therefore, a serious Doha round package would deliver substantially lower developed-country barriers to developing-country exports of agriculture and manufactures, stronger liberalization commitments by advanced developing countries, stronger developed- and developing-country commitments on trade in services, and some strengthening of WTO rules (e.g., on anti-dumping). More specifically, the EU would have to make further concessions on agricultural market access (tariff reductions and strict limits on exemptions for "sensitive products"). The United States would have to reciprocate with bigger cuts in domestic farm subsidies. Advanced developing countries, especially Brazil and India, would have to narrow the gap between bound and applied tariffs in agricultural and nonagricultural goods, concede net liberalization in some products, and restrict the range of "special products" exempted from agricultural liberalization. They would also have to make bigger concessions on "commercial presence" (i.e., foreign investment) in key services sectors. Finally, developed countries would have to make some concessions on Mode Four in services (cross-border movement of temporary workers).

A big success was never a realistic prospect. Rather, in a climate of all-around defensiveness, most players seemed to converge on a midget of a deal that would have delivered very little net liberalization. But this foundered on U.S. resistance: it had always insisted on a substantial deal, with significant access to advanced developing-country markets in return for U.S. concessions on farm subsidies and other items.

The apparent collapse of the Doha round leaves the WTO in very serious trouble. But a midget deal would not make matters better. The widespread perception is that multilateral liberalization is going nowhere; there will be much greater temptation to unpick existing agreements and flout multilateral rules; many more sensitive cases will be taken to dispute settlement, which will come under greater political strain; action will switch further and decisively to PTAs; and the world trading system will be shaped more by a messy patchwork of PTAs driven by power politics than by fair and balanced multilateral rules.

All the WTO's structural problems described earlier have played into the miserable failure of the Doha round. This leaves the WTO drifting inexorably in all the wrong directions—toward the easy politics of a UN-style talking shop and a World Bank–style aid agency for developing-country basket cases (through aid-for-trade and other initiatives that have consumed as much attention as market-access negotiations), and ever further away from the hard politics of liberalization and the rules that underpin it. Will the collapse of the round concentrate minds among the players who count? Might it induce them to get real, get back to basics, stop the rot, and set the WTO on its legs again?

The Future of the WTO

W. B. Yeats wrote that when things fall apart, the center cannot hold. Looking beyond the Doha round, what, if anything, can hold the WTO and the multilateral trading system together? The answer must be to recognize and tackle the WTO's systemic problems—the underlying causes of Doha round malaise.

To get the WTO out of its rut, its members need to do three things: restore focus on a core market-access and rules agenda, that is, progressive liberalization of trade barriers, underpinned by transparent, nondiscriminatory rules; revive effective decisionmaking; and, not least, scale back ambitions and expectations.

First, a market-access and rules focus would be traditionalist in the sense that it would restore a GATT-like compass to the WTO. But it could not and would not be a return to a golden yesterday. A post-GATT agenda would have to range wider (broader sectoral coverage than the GATT) and venture deeper (procedural disciplines to make trade-related domestic regulations more transparent and nondiscriminatory)—but without regulatory overload and a top-down standards-harmonization agenda. It is a question of finding a balance: one that would have a lowest common denominator of rules and obligations applicable to a critical mass of WTO members, but still one that would allow wide room for national policy and institutional choice. This scenario would be sufficiently open-ended to encourage bottom-up unilateral experimentation in response to local circumstances and challenges. This would, in turn, promote a decentralized, marketlike competitive emulation among governments in search of better practice.

Within this frame, a post-Doha agenda should shift emphasis from liberalization to rules. The Doha round has shown that substantial multilateral liberalization will be elusive in the future. That still leaves other liberalizing avenues, notably PTAs and unilateral measures. More important than further multilateral liberalization is safeguarding multilateral rules for open and stable international commerce. These rules, on tariff and nontariff measures, at and behind the border, are indispensable. But they are under threat as a result of WTO malfunction. They can be safeguarded and updated only in a multilateral forum, not unilaterally, bilaterally or in regional clubs. Developed countries and advanced developing countries need them to guarantee access to each other's markets. Poorer and weaker developing countries would be squeezed out and further marginalized without them. Given these common stakes, and once the dust of the Doha round has settled, rules issues should take priority over further multilateral liberalization.[5]

Second, nothing of substance can be achieved without mending the WTO's broken decisionmaking mechanism. This does not depend fundamentally on reforming formal procedures; there is no chance of consensus on major internal reforms, and it would be a distraction from more important matters. Rather, effective decisionmaking depends on intergovernmental political will and *informal* decisionmaking. This requires recognition of hard-boiled realities outside Geneva. About 50 countries (30 if the EU is counted as 1) account for well over 80 percent of international trade and an even greater share of foreign direct investment.[6] This comprises the OECD plus about 20 developing countries that have been globalizing rapidly and successfully (most of them in Asia, some in Latin America, and very few in Africa). These are the ones with workable governments, sufficient appreciation of their own interests, negotiating capacity, and bargaining power. They need to strike the key liberalizing and rule-making deals. They must be active individually and in multi-country coalitions, ranging from informal, broad-based coalitions to smaller, issue-based ones such as the Cairns Group and the G-20 on agriculture and "Friends Groups" on other issues.

Within this outer core, there is an inner core of "big beasts": the United States and EU, of course, but now joined by the increasingly influential developing-country majors, India, China, and Brazil. Japan should be there too, but it punches well below its weight in the WTO. The old understanding of an EU–United States duopoly driving the GATT/WTO enterprise no longer works. No doubt, the EU will continue to be a WTO heavyweight, and transatlantic cooperation will remain vital. But the EU's leadership credentials are not great. In the WTO, it is too defensive on agriculture and too offensive in trying to push dubious new regulation on environmental standards and other issues. On the wider global stage, it cannot surpass the United States, and the rising powers in Asia-Pacific are catching up. More important for the WTO's future will be clearer, up-front U.S. leadership and constructive participation by China, India, Brazil, and perhaps Japan. Of the developing-country majors, China's role will be most important. Ultimately, in the absence of leadership by the big beasts, nothing in the WTO will move.

These inner and outer cores must concentrate primarily on core market access in agriculture, nonagricultural goods and services, and related core rules (including anti-dumping, safeguards, subsidies, regional trade agreements, and dispute settlement). New issues (such as the Singapore issues and trade-and-environment) should be dealt with plurilaterally through opt-ins or opt-outs. This would give developing countries the cushion to join negotiations only if and when they feel ready to do so.

That leaves about 100 poorer and weaker developing countries—two-thirds of the membership. In Geneva, the conventional wisdom is that they can and should participate actively in collective decision-making, with the help of technical assistance and associated "capacity building" provided by international organizations and national donors. This is therapeutic multilateralism. It is fanciful, indeed utopian.

These countries must of course be consulted and will exercise influence through the African Least Developed Countries; African, Caribbean and Pacific Group of States; G-90; and other "common-characteristic" groupings. But the plain fact is that they are very marginally involved in the world economy, and most have chronic misgovernment that often descends into ethnic strife, civil war, and state collapse. Negotiating resources are also scarce, and there is little ability and political will to implement WTO agreements. Hence, these countries are unable to play more than a secondary and reactive role in the WTO. They exercise "negative" bargaining power, that is, they can and do block negotiations. But, frankly, they are incapable of exercising much "positive" bargaining power in the foreseeable future. As is abundantly clear in the Doha round, they demand entitlements (such as maintenance of their tariff preferences and increased aid) but are not in a position to make credible negotiating proposals of their own.

Providing these countries do not block negotiations, they should be accorded generous old-style special and differential treatment—essentially a free ride. Through most favored nation status, they should have rights to whatever liberalization is negotiated by others, and preferably duty and quota-free access to OECD and leading developing-country markets. At the same time, they should not be obliged to reciprocate with their own liberalization, nor should they be under pressure to sign up for other new obligations if they feel unready to do so. There should be a "peace clause" on dispute settlement: an understanding that they will not be taken to court, even if in breach of existing obligations. These terms should not pose a problem for the core group of 50 (or 30). The rest of the WTO membership are of minimal commercial interest and not of significant strategic political interest to the major developed- and developing-country powers.

Practical politics dictates that such a two-tier or multitier configuration should not be expressed in formal WTO decisionmaking procedures. That would be unacceptable to the majority of the membership outside the outer core. It would be needlessly divisive. Rather, the key decisions must be taken informally in smaller, self-selecting groups, followed by broader multilateral consultations and some (but not unlimited) diplomatic give-and-take.

Third, given its huge political complications, the WTO must adapt to a more modest future. Even with the right dose of realism, there are *narrower* limits and diminishing returns to GATT/WTO-style multilateralism—for the reasons discussed earlier. Post-Doha, market-access, and rule-making negotiations should be more cautious and incremental, and trade rounds should probably become a thing of the past. Cautious incrementalism should apply particularly to negotiating further liberalization, where the political roadblocks are biggest. More priority should be given instead to safeguarding, updating, and administering multilateral trade rules. There should be more emphasis on the WTO as an OECD-type forum to share information and ideas, and to improve transparency through mutual policy surveillance, especially for developing countries. Finally, in the absence of a powerful negotiating mechanism, dispute settlement should be exercised with judicial restraint and not extended further. It would be politically illegitimate and counterproductive to advance multilateralism through international public law without an underlying international political consensus. That is just the sort of global-governance hubris to avoid.

Finally, let us look at the WTO in a "constitutional" light. Many call for the WTO, and other international organizations, to become more "democratic," "inclusive," and "participatory." They argue that participation in decisionmaking should be open to nongovernmental actors, whether from organized business, labor, or NGOs. Wider participation, beyond the confines of an intergovernmental club, is needed to make collective decisions "legitimate."[7]

This view reflects an ancient Greek notion of democracy—Benjamin Constant's "liberty of the ancients." In modern guise, the argument is that established political institutions, at national and international levels, are not representative enough: decisionmaking has to be shared more widely. But it is ahistorical, unempirical, indeed hopelessly naive, to expect masses of individuals in complex societies to make informed collective choices, even in advanced liberal democracies. That is true at the national level. It is even truer of international institutions, far removed from the daily ken and concerns of ordinary people. "Participatory democracy" would end up giving free rein to the passions and tyranny of the minorities—a cornucopia of well-organized special interests who would hijack political systems and weigh them down with multiple and conflicting objectives.

Many of these organized interests share a profound distrust of the market economy and a faith in government command-and-control mechanisms. That is certainly true of most NGOs swirling around the WTO. Their economically nonsensical arguments against trade liberalization and associated market-based reforms in developing countries have been a notable feature of the Doha round. They have forged alliances with the governments of poorer (particularly African) developing countries with scant negotiating resources, and have significantly influenced their defensive, one-sided, and ultimately untenable negotiating positions. At Ministerial Conferences, they have encouraged and sometimes orchestrated tactics to block negotiations. A major fault line in the WTO is its seemingly limitless indulgence of so-called civil society. It is regrettable that the barbarians have been allowed inside the gates and given license to vandalize the grounds and wreck the furniture.[8]

Of course these tendencies derail effective decisionmaking and liberalization in the WTO. More fundamentally, they undermine modern constitutional liberalism. The latter's central insight is that democracy has to be checked, balanced, and delegated if it is not to trample on the freedom of the individual and degenerate into the tyranny of majorities and minorities. Liberty has to be protected *against* democracy and its offspring of overactive government. This is James Madison's and Alexander Hamilton's legacy to the American Republic they helped to found, as embodied in the U.S. Constitution and interpreted in *The Federalist Papers*. It applies as much to international politics as it does to national politics. The WTO should be no exception.

The WTO's central objective should be to facilitate the ongoing liberalization of international commerce with workable rules. That is a libertarian objective, not a democratic one, for it presupposes the protection of individuals' freedom to transact across borders. It also presupposes limited, not open-ended, government. That demands classical liberal–type rules: simple, transparent, nondiscriminatory "negative ordinances" that protect individual property rights *against* government intervention.[9] Within national jurisdictions, such rules are embodied in private (commercial) law. Their external complements are Articles I and III of the GATT (on most favored nation and national treatment, respectively).[10] The point of the old GATT was for governments to collectively tie their hands with rules to limit their interventions and give more sway to the market economy, albeit in a limited policy arena. A "democratic" WTO would probably go in a different direction. It would likely lead to a raft of detailed, prescriptive regulations that would increase government intervention and restrict economic freedom.[11]

Conclusion

The WTO's raison d'être is to provide a framework of rules to assist (mainly developing-country) governments that have strategically chosen to take their national economies in a market-oriented, globally integrated direction. That demands willing adherence to WTO rules. The problem with the Doha round is that it has become home and breeding ground to a swarm of anti-market ideas and activity that defeat the very purpose of the WTO. A majority of developing-country governments, egged on by anti-market NGOs, expect Northern liberalization while insisting on wholesale exemptions from WTO rules themselves, in addition to their inevitable demands for more aid. Developed-country governments are equally to blame for not countering these arguments and for mollifying, instead of confronting, "civil society," inside and outside the WTO. In essence, they are culpable because they have failed to make the case for global markets and the multilateral rules that strengthen them.

Political realism is also in order—something from which the WTO has taken an extended vacation. The WTO has to work with the grain of global political and economic realities if it is to work at all. That means U.S. leadership, cooperation among major powers, and "coalitions of the willing" among the approximately 50 WTO members who count. As Martin Wolf says, "The trick of making multilateral institutions work is to recognise the realities of power, without succumbing entirely to them."[12] Furthermore, political realism demands future modesty, especially in scaling down ambitions for further multilateral liberalization, with correspondingly more focus on defending sensible and workable multilateral trade rules. The latter is more important than the former.

Cassandras would conclude that the WTO has already crossed the Rubicon to a permanent state of UN-style infantilism and that it is incapable of crossing Joseph Conrad's "shadow line"—from a world of callow irresponsibility to an adult world of real, solid, fixed things. Cautious optimists, however, would say that with more modest goals and proportionate means in a restricted intergovernmental setting, the WTO might be salvageable. It might just get back to being a helpful auxiliary to national market-based reforms, while avoiding pitfalls ahead, such as the danger of it becoming an EU-style regulatory agency saddled with an overloaded agenda or a UN-style development agency disbursing aid and rules carve-outs to developing countries.

5. Preferential Trade Agreements

We will work with can-do, not won't-do, countries.

—Robert Zoellick

All hat and no cattle.

—Texan saying

Given the parlous state of the World Trade Organization, it is not surprising that governments all over the world have turned to bilateral and regional negotiations to conclude preferential (i.e., discriminatory) trade agreements. These, it is said, can move faster, wider, deeper than multilateral negotiations. Thus, venting his spleen after the WTO's failed Cancún Ministerial Conference, Bob Zoellick, the U.S. special trade representative, promised to speed ahead with bilateral deals with willing "can-do" partners. Skeptics, however, say that preferential trade agreements (PTAs) are not what they are cracked up to be. And cynics would echo the Texanism quoted above.

Do PTAs facilitate regional economic integration and, by extension, global economic integration? How credible are negotiating positions, the choice of negotiating partners, and the agreements already in operation? How good or bad is the fit between PTAs and economic policy at home? And how do they relate to involvement in the WTO? Take a look first at general trends, and then at PTAs in Asia, the scene of the most feverish PTA activity in recent years.

Building Blocs and Stumbling Blocs

By July 2005, 330 PTAs had been notified to the General Agreement on Tariffs and Trade/WTO—206 of them since the establishment

Figure 5.1
REGIONAL TRADE AGREEMENTS IN FORCE BY DATE OF ENTRY INTO
FORCE, 1948–2004

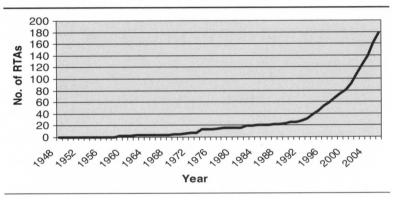

SOURCE: WTO, www.wto.org/english/tratop_e/region_e/summary_e.
xls.

of the WTO in 1995 (Figure 5.1). More than 180 are in force, with
many more expected to be operational soon. Of the PTAs in force,
84 percent are free trade agreements (FTAs), with customs unions
and partial-scope agreements making up the rest.[1] Bilateral (country-
to-country) agreements account for over 75 percent of PTAs in force
and almost 90 percent of those under negotiation. PTA activity has
increased pace since 1999–2000, and even more so since the launch
of the Doha round.[2]

Many regions have long been involved in PTAs. For the European
Union, this goes back to its beginnings in the European Coal and
Steel Community and then the European Economic Community. In
North America, it took off with the U.S.-Canada FTA in the late
1980s. Africa, Latin America, and south Asia got going in the 1960s,
and eastern Europe and the ex–Soviet Union after the end of the
cold war.

East Asia was the conspicuous exception: it tended to rely more
on nondiscriminatory unilateral and multilateral liberalization. Now
it is playing catch-up, with PTA initiatives spreading like wildfire
in the past six years (Figure 5.2; see Figure 5.3 on the PTA network
in the wider Asia-Pacific region). This has mostly taken the form of
bilateral FTAs rather than plurilateral or regional negotiations. The
major Asian powers—China, India, and Japan—are involved, as are

Figure 5.2
PTAs in East Asia

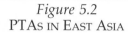

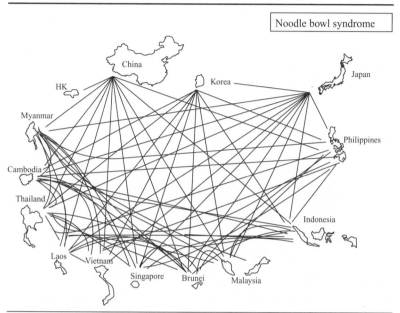

Source: R. Baldwin, "Managing the Noodle Bowl: The Fragility of East Asian Regionalism," January 2006, www.sussex.ac.uk/Units/caris/CARIS/T. Carpenter-R.Baldwin-Sussex%20RTA%20Conference-Manage_CEPR_DP.pdf.

Note: The map shows FTAs signed or under negotiation in January 2006. East Asia is defined here as the 10 ASEANs, China, Japan, and South Korea.

South Korea, Australia, New Zealand, Hong Kong, the southeast Asian countries (grouped in ASEAN—the Association of Southeast Asian Nations), as well as other south Asian countries. As of 2005, ASEAN as a regional grouping, China, and India were involved in 7, 9, and 15 FTA agreements or negotiations, respectively. If individual ASEAN-member FTA initiatives are counted, there are about 20 FTAs in force and 60 more in the pipeline in China, India, and southeast Asia. The United States is involved with individual countries in east Asia, as are some Latin American countries (notably Mexico, Chile, and more recently Brazil). South Africa is considering initiatives in the region. Of the major powers, only the EU remained outside the fray of PTA activity in Asia—until it changed its policy

Figure 5.3
PTAS IN ASIA-PACIFIC

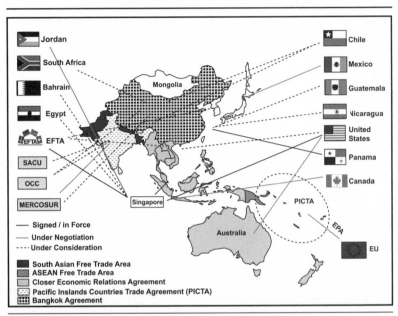

SOURCE: R. Sen, "ASEAN's Bilateral Preferential Trade and Economic Cooperation Agreements: Evolution, Characteristics and Implications for Economic Integration," 2006. GCC = Gulf Cooperation Council; MERCOSUR = Southern Common Market; SACU = Southern African Customs Union.

in late 2006. EU FTA negotiations with India, ASEAN, and South Korea started in 2007.[3]

Modern economic arguments pro and contra PTAs spring from Jacob Viner's classic distinction between trade creation and trade diversion. (The former results from a shift in production from a high-cost member to a low-cost member of a PTA, and the latter from a diversion of imports from a low-cost nonmember to a high-cost member of a PTA.) Now more complex models examine investment effects, economies of scale, and assorted dynamic (longer-run) effects. The political-economy discussion of PTAs revolves around their roles as "building blocs" or "stumbling blocs" to multilateral liberalization. This has become part of trade-policy duckspeak.[4]

Why this rush of recent PTA activity?[5] Foreign policy considerations loom large. PTAs are viewed as a means of cementing stronger political (as well as economic) links with favored partners, for example, as a door opener to other strategic, security-related agreements. This is clearly the case with Singapore, for example, particularly its FTA with the United States. On the economic front, PTAs are a response to stalled multilateral liberalization and a weak WTO. Indeed, they are seen as insurance policies against continuing WTO weakness: they secure *preferential* access to major markets and are a means of managing and defusing trade tensions with powerful players.

Not surprisingly, governments tend to present PTAs in a positive light. They are seen as part of a benign "competitive-liberalization" process. PTAs among small clubs of like-minded countries can, they argue, take liberalization and regulatory reform further than would be the case in a large, heterogeneous, and unwieldy WTO. This can, in turn, stimulate multilateral liberalization.

For PTAs to make economic sense, they should have comprehensive sectoral coverage, be consistent with relevant WTO provisions (in GATT Article XXIV and General Agreement on Trade in Services Article V), and preferably go beyond both WTO commitments and applied practice at home. In other words, they should involve genuine and tangible, not bogus, liberalization. There should be strong provisions for nonborder regulatory cooperation, especially to improve transparency in domestic laws and regulations to facilitate market access and boost competition. Rules-of-origin (ROOs) requirements should be as simple, generous, and harmonized as possible to minimize trade diversion and red tape.[6] Strong, clean "WTO-plus" PTAs should reinforce domestic economic and institutional reforms to remove market distortions and extend competition. Finally, nonpreferential (most favored nation [MFN]) tariffs should be low to minimize any trade diversion resulting from PTAs.

All this presupposes a sense of economic strategy when entering into PTA negotiations—choosing negotiating partners and assessing the costs and benefits of negotiating positions, and how they relate to the WTO and to the national economic-policy framework. A sense of strategy, with careful preparation through research, analysis, and reflection, is even more important for key PTA negotiations and subsequent implementation than it is in the WTO. Bilateral negotiations with major powers—especially with the United States and the EU—are much more issue- and resource-intensive than WTO negotiations. They demand better preparation and coordination across different agencies within government, and between government and nongovernmental constituencies, especially business.

Unfortunately, the characterization above is the exception, not the rule, of PTAs in practice. The EU, the North American Free Trade Agreement, and the Australia–New Zealand Closer Economic Relations Trade Agreement are the exceptions. They have zero tariffs and quotas on all (or almost all) intra-PTA goods trade; comprehensive coverage of services trade and of cross-border investment (in goods and services); WTO-plus commitments on cross-border labor movement (essentially free movement of labor in the EU and ANZC-ERTA); WTO-plus commitments on government procurement, trade facilitation, and competition rules; strong disciplines and intensive cooperation on all manner of nonborder trade-related regulation; and, not least, low average MFN tariffs that reduce trade diversion.

However, most other FTAs and customs unions are weak, often falling short of WTO provisions. This is particularly true of South-South PTAs (i.e., between developing countries), but also holds for many North-South PTAs. These tend to be driven by foreign policy aspirations, but with justifications that are all too often vague, muddled, and trivial, having little relevance to commercial realities and the economic nuts and bolts of trade agreements. This can amount to little more than symbolic copycatting of other countries' PTA activity and otherwise empty-gesture politics. In such cases, economic strategy is conspicuous by its absence.

The predictable results of foreign policy–driven PTA negotiations light on economic strategy are bitty, quick-fix sectoral deals. Politically sensitive sectors in goods and services are carved out, as are crucial areas where progress in the WTO is elusive (especially disciplines on anti-dumping duties and agricultural subsidies). Little progress is usually made in tackling domestic regulatory barriers (e.g., relating to investment, competition, government procurement, trade facilitation, cross-border labor movement, and food-safety and technical standards). These PTAs hardly go beyond WTO commitments; deliver little, if any, net liberalization and pro-competitive regulatory reform; and get tied up in knots of restrictive, overlapping rules of origin. Especially for developing countries with limited negotiating capacity, resource-intensive PTA negotiations risk diverting political and bureaucratic attention from the WTO and from necessary domestic reforms. Finally, the sway of power politics can result in highly asymmetrical deals, especially when one of the negotiating parties is a major player.

The United States eschews such a "trade-light" approach, advertising strong, comprehensive, WTO-plus FTAs. This normally entails major concessions by its negotiating partners, but few U.S. concessions—as the FTAs now in force with Australia and Singapore demonstrate. U.S. FTAs have wide and deep coverage of goods, services, and investment, with strong disciplines to limit domestic regulatory discretion and to improve transparency; very strong intellectual property protection; mutual recognition agreements on standards and professional qualifications; disciplines on government procurement, trade facilitation, and competition rules; provisions for temporary movement of businesspeople; and (fairly weak) commitments on labor and environmental standards. The edifice is underpinned by strong dispute settlement, including investor-state dispute settlement, and mechanisms for intensive regulatory cooperation. However, there are weaker disciplines or carve-outs for some politically sensitive sectors (particularly in U.S. agriculture); no WTO-plus disciplines on agricultural subsidies or anti-dumping measures; and often complicated and restrictive rules of origin.

Latin America, Africa, the Middle East, and the ex–Soviet Union now contain a hotchpotch of weak and partial PTAs. The average African country belongs to four different agreements, and the average Latin American country belongs to seven. (See Figures 5.4 and 5.5, respectively, for maps of PTAs in Africa and the Americas.) Overlapping PTAs have different tariff schedules, ROOs, and implementation periods. This is exacerbated by poor implementation and relatively high MFN tariffs. The Commonwealth of Independent States, the Common Market of Eastern and Southern Africa, the Southern African Development Community, the East African Community, the West African Economic and Monetary Union, and the South Asian Advanced Regional Co-Operation Agreement (now the South Asian Free Trade Area) are such examples. They could cost more in lost trade revenues than they gain from tariff preferences.

Restrictive ROOs are especially troubling. EU, U.S., and NAFTA ROOs differ considerably from one another, and have different rules for different products (combining two or more criteria in myriad ways). For instance, NAFTA ROOs may be equivalent to a tariff of

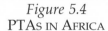

Figure 5.4
PTAs in Africa

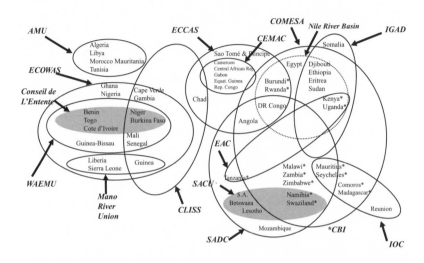

SOURCE: World Bank, "Regional Trade Agreements and Development: Upside Potential and Downside Risks," Trade Note 24, September 13, 2005, http://siteresources.worldbank.org/INTRANETTRADE/Resources/239054-1126812419270/TradeNote24_Newfarmer.pdf.

4.3 percent, and they could be the main factor in the limited effect of NAFTA on Mexican exports. Other PTAs, for example, the ASEAN Free Trade Area, the Common Market of Eastern and Southern Africa, and the Economic Community of West African States, have less restrictive ROOs. But nearly all South-South PTAs have significant product-specific exemptions from uniform ROO criteria, a tendency to increasing product-specific ROO complexity, and high-cost certification procedures to determine the origin of goods.[7]

More generally, complex ROO requirements make no sense in a world where production of goods (and, increasingly, services) is fragmented, with different parts of the value chain located in different countries, and then integrated across borders through trade in

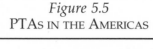

Figure 5.5
PTAs in the Americas

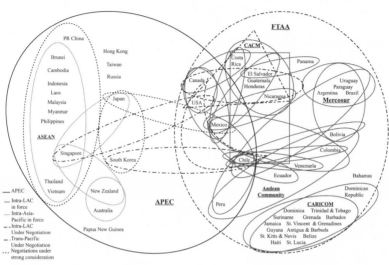

Source: R. Devlin and A. Estevadeordal, "Trade and Cooperation: A Regional Public Goods Approach," draft, Inter-American Development Bank, Washington, DC, 2002, www.pecc.org/trade/papers/vancouver-2002/estevadeordal.pdf.

components and other intermediate products. Inputs are sourced from many different countries that can supply them at lowest cost. Only then can exports be competitive. Globalization accelerates this process, but complex ROOs in several, overlapping PTAs throw a monkey wrench in the works. Even subtle differences in rules of origin can raise business costs and divert trade and associated investment. These costs are much more onerous for small and medium-sized trading firms in developing countries than they are for large corporations in developed countries.

Is this PTA "spaghetti bowl" in danger of being replicated in Asia? Or are the new Asian PTAs more serious? Do they hold out the prospect of strengthening regional and global integration? Now let us look at the PTA activity of the major Asian players: China, the ASEAN countries, India, Japan, and South Korea.

PTAs in Asia[8]

The Main Players: China, ASEAN, India, Japan, and South Korea

China is the driving force for PTAs in Asia. It is considering or negotiating FTAs left, right, and center—in east and south Asia, the Middle East, Latin America, and Africa, and with Australia and New Zealand. By 2006, it had 9 FTAs on the books and was considering negotiations with up to 30 other countries.

Its core FTA strategy is directed at its close neighborhood. Politically, China would like to use FTAs to establish leadership credentials in east Asia. On the economic front, strong Chinese FTAs with regional partners might make sense, given ever-closer trade-and-investment linkages in northeast and southeast Asia, particularly involving global manufacturing supply chains. The problem is that the region subsumes a diverse array of economies with big pockets of protection here and there. Opening to trade with China would leave several sheltered sectors exposed, such as agriculture in Japan and South Korea and agriculture, textiles, and clothing in the lesser-developed ASEAN countries (Indonesia, the Philippines, Cambodia, Laos, Vietnam, and Myanmar). Extreme agricultural protection in Japan and South Korea will make comprehensive China-Japan and China–South Korea FTAs almost impossible to negotiate.

The China-ASEAN set of negotiations, more than any other FTA initiative, is the one to watch in the region. The aim is to have an FTA in place by 2010. It would be the largest FTA ever negotiated, covering 11 diverse economies with a population of 1.7 billion and a gross domestic product of US$2 trillion. There has been reasonable progress in eliminating tariffs on trade in goods, but little progress to date has been made on nontariff barriers in goods, services (where a relatively weak agreement has been reached), investment, and other issues. China also has relatively strong, WTO-plus FTAs with Hong Kong and Macao (both admittedly special cases) and a comprehensive FTA on goods with Chile (though that is all it covers to date), and it is negotiating FTAs with Australia and New Zealand. It is also negotiating or thinking of negotiating rather weak FTAs elsewhere in the developing world, for example, with Pakistan,

MERCOSUR (the Southern Common Market), the South African Customs Union, and perhaps India. These are shallow—mostly preferential tariff reductions on a limited range of products.

In all, China is making the running on FTAs in Asia. Its approach is pragmatic and eclectic, ranging from strong (Hong Kong and Macao) to middling-to-weak (probably ASEAN) to very weak (probably India, the South African Customs Union, and other countries in Africa, the Middle East, and elsewhere). Even the China-ASEAN FTA is unlikely to create much extra trade and investment if it does not go substantially beyond tariff elimination in goods. Trading interests are placed in the context of foreign policy "soft power," that is, diplomacy and relationship building. Though China is a little more serious about FTAs than most other regional players, its FTAs are driven more by "high politics" (competition with Japan to establish leadership credentials in east Asia and securing of privileged influence in other regions) than economic strategy. The danger is that this will deliver weak, partial FTAs that create little trade but a lot more political and economic complications. And that would send powerful signals to other countries to do the same.

Turning to southeast Asia, Singapore blazed the FTA trail, with Thailand next to follow, and now Malaysia, Indonesia, the Philippines, and Vietnam trying to catch up. Singapore has agreements in force with Australia, New Zealand, Japan, the United States, South Korea, India, and a host of other minor trading partners, and several others proposed or under negotiation in Africa, the Middle East, south Asia, and the Americas. Thailand has agreements in force with Australia, New Zealand, Bahrain, China, and India, and one concluded with Japan. It was in negotiations with the United States and others, before the Thai political crisis and the subsequent military coup put all negotiations on hold. Malaysia has an agreement with Japan, and is negotiating with the United States, Australia, New Zealand, India, Pakistan, South Korea, and Chile. The Philippines and Indonesia have new FTAs with Japan, and both are looking to start negotiations with others. Vietnam has a bilateral trade agreement with the United States, is negotiating with Japan, and is considering other negotiations. In addition, ASEAN collectively has negotiations with China, India, Japan, Australia–New Zealand CER, and South Korea. ASEAN-EU FTA negotiations started in 2007.

Of the ASEAN countries, only Singapore has reasonably strong FTAs, and an especially strong FTA with the United States with comprehensive coverage and strong rules for goods, services, investment, and other issues. But Singapore, with its free-port economy, centralized city-state politics, efficient administration, and world-class regulatory standards, is a misleading indicator for the region. Thailand provides a better indicator. Its FTAs were rushed; too many negotiations were launched; and they proceeded too fast, with little overarching strategy. The residual FTA logic was narrowly mercantilist: export market access in a few sectors was sought in return for import concessions in a few others, while otherwise preserving the domestic-protectionist status quo. This trade-light approach has resulted in weak FTAs that will make little positive difference to competition and efficiency in the Thai economy, but will create complications in the process (not least with a bewildering array of rules-of-origin requirements). The U.S.-Thai FTA was likely to be the sole exception due to American demands for wide and deep commitments. But negotiations ran into serious domestic opposition in Thailand, before being derailed by the Thai political crisis and subsequent military coup.

Thus far, most signs point to ASEAN countries becoming entangled in a web of weak and partial FTAs. Many product areas, especially in agriculture, are likely to be excluded from goods liberalization. Regulatory barriers are unlikely to be tackled with disciplines that go much deeper than existing WTO commitments. Services commitments are unlikely to advance much beyond the WTO's General Agreement on Trade in Services, let alone deliver meaningful net liberalization or regulatory cooperation (e.g., on mutual recognition of standards and professional qualifications). Provisions on investment and the temporary movement of workers are also likely to be weak, with perhaps even weaker commitments on government procurement, competition rules, and customs administration.

More important than all the considerations above, it is already apparent that agreements in force and those being negotiated are creating a "noodle bowl" of complex and restrictive ROOs. A jumble of differing general and product-specific ROO criteria is emerging. These differ between bilateral FTAs. Collective ASEAN FTAs with third countries will compound the problem, if (as is quite likely) they end up with yet another layer of differing ROO criteria. If this is indeed what emerges, administrative and other compliance costs could be too onerous for most exporters in the region. Many will find it cheaper to pay the MFN-tariff duty. Little trade (and associated foreign direct investment) will be created, but there will be more work for customs officials.

India is also newly active with FTAs, in its south Asian backyard and in other developing-country regions. In south Asia, it has several bilateral FTAs. Hitherto loose regional cooperation is supposed to be transformed into the South Asian FTA by 2010, leading to a customs union by 2015 and economic union (whatever that means) by 2020. This looks unachievable in practice. For starters, the South Asia Free Trade Agreement excludes Indo-Pakistani trade. Planned negotiations are only on goods; they do not cover services, investment, and other nonborder market access issues. There are bound to be plenty of exemptions, given similar trade structures with competing products (especially in agriculture). Finally, severe political problems in the region (the Indo-Pakistani conflict over Kashmir, and the fact that India is completely surrounded by weak, failing, or failed states) will make progress very difficult.

India's approach to FTAs outside south Asia is mostly about foreign policy and is trade light, with little economic sense or strategy. An FTA with ASEAN is planned for completion by 2011, and bilateral FTAs are also in place with Thailand and Singapore. ASEAN-India and India-Thailand negotiations have been bedeviled by India's insistence on exempting swathes of products and on very restrictive rules of origin for products covered. In addition, India is part of the BIMSTEC (Bay of Bengal Initiative for Multi-Sectoral Technical and Economic Cooperation) group (the other members being Bangladesh, Sri Lanka, Nepal, Bhutan, Thailand, and Myanmar) that plans an FTA by 2017. It has mini-FTAs—basically limited tariff-concession schemes—in force or planned with several countries and regions, for example, Chile, the Southern African Customs Union, MERCOSUR (Southern Common Market), and IBSA (India, Brazil, and South Africa). FTA negotiations have started with Japan and South Korea and the EU.

Japan was the last major trading nation to hold out against discriminatory trade agreements, preferring the nondiscriminatory WTO track instead. This has changed decisively in the past five years.

Japan's biggest FTA initiative is the Japan-ASEAN Economic Partnership Agreement, which is supposed to be completed by 2012. It is comprehensive on paper, covering goods, services, investment, trade facilitation, and several areas for economic cooperation. However, progress has been slow—much slower than in the China-ASEAN FTA. This is due to Japanese reluctance to reduce and then phase out agricultural tariffs and to its insistence on restrictive and often product-specific rules of origin, especially for agricultural products (though for some manufacturing products as well). Another complicating factor is that Japan has given greater priority to bilateral FTA negotiations with individual ASEAN countries. Such bilateralism, especially with its noodle-bowl profusion of rules of origin, is going to make it very hard to achieve a clean, comprehensive Japan-ASEAN FTA. The latter risks ending up as a loose umbrella for a series of bilateral FTAs.

Japan has several other FTA initiatives in train. It calls its FTAs "economic partnership agreements" to indicate that they go beyond traditional FTAs in goods and have comprehensive coverage of trade and investment-related issues in goods and services. That is misleading: economic partnership agreements are euphemisms for weak and partial FTAs. In essence, Japan seems to be reacting to China's FTA advance, but without a real strategy.

South Korea is also in the thick of FTA activity. Like Japan, it is defensive on agriculture. Unlike Japan, it seems to be more serious on other negotiating issues. It has made more progress than Japan in FTA negotiations with ASEAN. South Korea and U.S. negotiators concluded an FTA in April 2007. Negotiations with the EU started in 2007.

Regional Economic Integration Initiatives

So much for bilateral FTAs in east and south Asia. Now look at broader regional economic-integration initiatives. These are Asia-Pacific Economic Cooperation and ASEAN initiatives, as well as pan–east Asian and pan-Asian FTA initiatives.

APEC's membership is diverse and unwieldy; its agenda has become impossibly broad and unfocused; its vaunted Open (i.e., nondiscriminatory) Regionalism is dead in the water; and these days, it is driven by shallow conferencitis and summitry. It cannot be expected to contribute anything serious to regional economic integration. An APEC FTA initiative (Free Trade Area of the Asia-Pacific) was launched at the APEC Hanoi Summit in 2006.[9] It will go nowhere: political and economic divisions in such a large, heterogeneous grouping are manifold and intractable.

In southeast Asia, the ASEAN Free Trade Area has an accelerated timetable for intra-ASEAN tariff elimination, but has seen little progress on "AFTA-plus" items, such as services, investment, nontariff barriers, and mutual recognition and harmonization of standards. An ASEAN Economic Community, a single market for goods, services, capital, and the movement of skilled labor, is supposed to be achieved by 2015. So far, however, ASEAN Vision Statements and other blueprints have largely failed to remove barriers to commerce in southeast Asia. They seem rather distant from commercial ground realities.

Finally, there is much talk in the region of folding bilateral and ASEAN FTAs into larger, integrated FTAs that would cover east Asia, and perhaps include south Asia too. An ASEAN Plus Three FTA (the "three" being Japan, South Korea, and China) has been touted, as has an east Asian FTA that might include Australia and New Zealand. There is talk of a pan-Asian FTA that would include India or the South Asia FTA. Visions of an East Asian Economic Community, and even an Asian Economic Community, have appeared on the horizon. The first East Asian Summit, held in Kuala Lumpur in November 2005, was supposed to get these bigger regional-integration efforts under way, at least for east Asia.

So far, this talk is loose and empty—nothing more. Regional players are speeding ahead with quick and dirty bilateral FTAs, while little progress is being made with the larger ASEAN FTAs (beyond tariff elimination in goods trade). The emerging pattern is of a patchwork of bilateral "hub-and-spoke" FTAs, in a noodle bowl of trade-restricting rules of origin. This threatens to slow down and distort the advance of regional and global production networks. In particular, it could undermine the dense networks of east Asian production sharing and trade in manufacturing parts and components ("fragmentation-based trade," or what Richard Baldwin calls "Factory Asia"), which are, in turn, linked to final export markets in Europe and North America.[10] Moreover, such FTA activity distracts attention from further unilateral liberalization and domestic reforms. That will probably hinder, not help, the cause of regional economic integration.

More generally, bitter nationalist rivalries (especially in northeast Asia and between India and Pakistan), and vast intercountry differences in economic structure, development, policies, and institutions, will continue to stymie Asian regional-integration efforts for a long time to come. This applies to east Asia, and it applies even more to south Asia.

Implications for Asia in the WTO

Frenetic PTA activity does raise questions about Asian countries' engagement in the WTO and their commitment to the multilateral trading system. Do PTAs reinforce Asian influence in the WTO? Or do they divert attention from it? What effect have they had on Asian participation in the Doha round?

Some Asian countries were active in the Uruguay round, though in different ways. India was archdefensive and led developing-country opposition to developed-country demands. Japan, at the other end, was an active *demandeur* in market-access and rules negotiations. South Korea, Hong Kong, the ASEAN countries, Australia, and New Zealand were newly active in the GATT, alongside their general shift to liberal, outward-oriented trade policies and their increasing integration into the world economy.

The Doha round picture looks very different. India has become even more active than it was in the Uruguay round, but Japan, South Korea, and the ASEAN countries have been visibly less active. Most conspicuously, Japan punches well below its economic weight in the WTO. Nearly all east Asian countries have diverted political attention and negotiating resources away from the WTO and toward FTAs. China is the major exception. Its WTO commitments are by far the strongest of any developing country in the WTO (of which more in the next chapter). As a result of its unilateral liberalization and WTO accession, China's levels of trade protection are rather low by developing-country standards, and it has acquired a strong stake in a rules-based multilateral trading system. Hence, it has been active in the Doha round, though in a quiet, behind-the-scenes manner.

The general east Asian neglect of the WTO is extremely myopic, and may prove to be a monumental miscalculation. The region needs an effective WTO. Its integration with the world economy gives it a long-term stake in a liberal trading system underpinned by strong, nondiscriminatory rules. A patchwork of overlapping and discriminatory FTAs is not enough and, in the absence of a healthy multilateral system, will probably be damaging. This logic applies compellingly to south Asian countries too, given their increasing integration into the world economy.

As discussed in the previous chapter, Japan, South Korea, Taiwan, Hong Kong, China, India, and the more advanced ASEAN members are in an outer core of about 50 countries (or 30 if the EU is counted as 1) that need to be active to restore the WTO's longer-term fortunes. And China, India, and perhaps Japan are in an inner core that needs to exercise leadership.

Conclusion

There is now a hearty appetite for PTAs in ever-bigger spaghetti bowls and noodle bowls. It will induce indigestion and worse. But it should not bring on apocalyptic visions of George Orwell's Oceania, Eastasia, and Eurasia, each hermetically sealed and at permanent war with the others. The global economy has become too integrated, and new intraregional and cross-regional PTAs too porous, to turn *1984* from fiction to reality, or indeed to presage a return to 1930s-style warring trade blocs. That, however, is no excuse for complacency.

Trade policy across the world is now highly unbalanced. It relies too much on (weak and partial) PTAs. This is likely to get worse with the unending stalemate or even collapse of the Doha round. PTAs are probably not going to tear down the remaining protectionist barriers that matter, whether in North-South or South-South commerce. Nearly all have the hallmarks of trade-light agreements. Some might even come close to being "trade-free" agreements. A blunt Texan would say that they are "all hat and no cattle." As Montaigne said of Seneca's writing, most of these PTAs make "more sound than sense," and some might even be "pure wind." Consequently, PTAs will not be the driving force of regional economic integration or further integration with the global economy. On the contrary, the emerging hub-and-spoke pattern of dirty FTAs threatens to be a force of economic disintegration—especially if the multilateral trading system weakens further.

However, FTAs are a reality; they cannot be wished away. But they can be improved, and they can fit better with trade policy on unilateral and multilateral tracks. That calls for comprehensive, WTO-plus FTAs with simple, harmonized ROOs. It is important to "multilateralize regionalism," for example, by simplifying and harmonizing ROOs and tariff schedules and (ideally) making preferences time limited (after which they would be open to all comers on a nondiscriminatory basis). If this does not happen, spaghetti bowls and noodle bowls threaten to undermine regional and global production networks.[11] But setting up and operating the requisite regional cooperation mechanisms will prove very difficult, given myriad political and economic divisions in east and south Asia— not to mention other developing-country regions.

Going about FTAs the wrong way—negotiating weak agreements with ROO complications that deflect attention from sensible unilateral reforms and the WTO—could easily lead to a world where most international trade would be governed by power relationships and arbitrary market-distorting preferences. Then the cornerstone of the multilateral trading system, the principle of nondiscrimination embodied in the GATT's MFN clause, would become more an abstraction than concrete reality. MFN treatment would end up as LFN—least favored nation treatment. This would make a mockery of comparative cost advantages, the foundation of sensible and mutually advantageous globalization.[12]

6. Asia, China, and Unilateral Liberalization

> *I trust the government . . . will not resume the policy which they and we have found most inconvenient, namely the haggling with foreign countries about reciprocal concessions, instead of taking that independent course which we believe to be conducive to our own interests. . . . Let us trust that our example, with the proof of practical benefits we derive from it, will at no remote period insure the adoption of the principles on which we have acted. . . . Let, therefore, our commerce be as free as our institutions. Let us proclaim commerce free, and nation after nation will follow our example.*

—Sir Robert Peel, announcing the repeal of the Corn Laws,
House of Commons, 1846

> *Liberalise first, negotiate later.*

—Mart Laar, ex–prime minister of Estonia

It is customary to look first to the World Trade Organization, or now to preferential trade agreements (PTAs), or to a combination of the two, to advance the liberalization of international commerce. This is questionable. As I have argued, the WTO today has severe limitations. So have PTAs. The transition from the General Agreement on Tariffs and Trade to the WTO has narrowed the possibilities for multilateral liberalization and rule strengthening—as the Doha round has amply demonstrated. And PTAs are unlikely to deliver large doses of additional liberalization, but will cause extra political and economic complications. Therefore, while trade negotiations have their place, they have distinct limits. Could it be that too much intellectual and political capital is invested in such top-down solutions? Do the solutions lie elsewhere? The quotes above point to a different route: *unilateral* liberalization by governments *outside* trade negotiations. Hence, this chapter begins with the political and economic feasibility of unilateral trade liberalization in the early 21st century.

The focus then switches to Asia, especially China. Like Rip Van Winkle, most of Asia slept through the global economic transformations of the last two centuries. That was particularly true of its political and populous giants, China and India. Now they have awoken and are finally integrating into the global economy; the next half century will see an Asian transformation of the global economy possibly as profound as that unleashed by the British-led Industrial Revolution. Unilateral liberalization of trade and foreign investment is central to this dynamic, and China is its driving force. Thus, the spotlight here falls on Asian—particularly Chinese—unilateral liberalization and its implications for trade policy worldwide.

The Political Economy of Unilateral Liberalization

The idea that a reasonably liberal international economic order can only be constructed by international organizations and intergovernmental negotiations is what I have called "liberalism from above." It stems from the interwar liberal-idealist tradition and became the established presumption with the post-1945 Bretton Woods and GATT settlements. Since then, it has been given intellectual respectability by the "liberal-internationalist" tradition in the academic study of international politics. Proponents hold that multiple points of friction between clashing government policies can and do descend into political and economic conflict, including protectionism. Negotiated intergovernmental cooperation in "international regimes," usually involving international organizations, is necessary to minimize conflict and keep the system open. This requires reciprocity, the exchange of concessions between governments through negotiation, not the "spontaneous" cooperation of governments unilaterally adapting their policies to changing international conditions. As Robert Axelrod and Robert Keohane put it, "Co-operation in world politics seems to be attained best not by providing benefits unilaterally to others, but by conditional cooperation."[1]

This approach was expedient to overcome the political and economic disasters between the two world wars and to deal with the reality that the United States, unlike 19th-century Britain, was unwilling to open its economy unconditionally after 1945. However, over time, liberalism from above has entrenched a misguided conventional wisdom, namely, that international institutions deliver trade liberalization "from outside," and only through "concessions" to foreigners in a game of haggling.

This has become central to the world view of international bureaucrats and politicians engaged in an endless round of conferences and summits. It tends to favor extra regulatory discretion, now at the international level, to intervene here or there, rather than "negative" international rules to limit government intervention and protect the individual's freedom to transact across national borders. At its extreme, it leads to an unconditional advocacy of international institutions. International cooperation—what is popularly called multilateralism—ends up as incantation and therapy rather than anything with intelligible meaning.[2] To adapt a Bushism, strong advocates consistently mis-overestimate the importance and effectiveness of international institutions, and are blind to their failings, such as excessive, self-serving bureaucracy and misguided meddling. The WTO and its Doha round are no exceptions. To the "WTO junkie," trade policy begins and ends in Geneva, and the WTO is the central trade pillar in the architecture of global governance. The Doha Development Agenda has been viewed as a means of delivering development (or salvation) "from above." Such are pipe dreams made of.

Liberalism from above overlooks fundamental lessons from theory, history, and the world around us today. Compelling political and economic arguments favor unilateral liberalization, with governments freeing up international trade and flows of capital and labor independently, not in the first instance via international negotiations. As any student of trade economics knows, welfare gains result directly from *import* liberalization, which replaces comparatively costly domestic production and reallocates resources more efficiently. It also spurs capital accumulation and economies of scale, as well as longer-run dynamic gains such as the transfer of technology and skills. Among its many benefits, import liberalization provides cheaper inputs and reallocates resources to promising export sectors. Similar and related arguments apply to the liberalization of inward investment and the cross-border movement of people.

Such gains come quicker through unconditional liberalization than through protracted, politicized, and bureaucratically cumbersome international negotiations. This Nike strategy ("Just Do It.") or, to use my alternative catch phrase, "liberalism from below," can make political sense too. Rather than relying on one-size-fits-all international blueprints, governments have the flexibility to initiate policies and emulate better practice abroad in experimental, trial-and-error fashion, tailored to specific local conditions. In this sense, a liberal trade order is not a "construct" of international negotiations; rather, it is *epiphenomenal*, a by-product of unilateral liberalization by one or several countries, progressively emulated by others.[3] In David Landes's words, it is "initiated from below and diffused by example." It induces an open-ended political (or institutional) competition among governments that allows them to spontaneously adjust to each other's practices in a world of uncertainty and flux, which enables them to adapt to overall change in the world economy in a relatively smooth and efficient manner. It is a dynamic, free-wheeling *marketlike* process, akin to F. A. Hayek's model of "competition as a discovery procedure."

Liberalism from below was the preferred method of the classical economists from Smith to Marshall and of the titans of mid-Victorian British politics. Britain did indeed lead the way with unilateral trade liberalization in the second half of the 19th century. In 20th- and 21st-century conditions of democratic politics, vigorous interest-group lobbying for protection, and ingrained mercantilist thinking, unilateral liberalization is of course a much more difficult proposition than it was in the 19th century. Hence the post-1945 logic of reciprocity. Until recently, multilateral reciprocity delivered the bulk of trade liberalization in the Organisation for Economic Co-operation and Development; and regional negotiations served the same purpose within the European Union. There were notable exceptions: Ludwig Erhard launched West Germany's domestic and foreign-economic liberalization unilaterally, which was partially imitated by other West European countries in the 1950s; and Japan, South Korea, and Taiwan pursued their selective trade-liberalization policies unilaterally too.

Since the 1980s, there has been a veritable trade-policy revolution outside the West, with region after region shifting from protection and isolation to freer trade and global economic integration. Observers often forget that this has come more "from below" than "from above." The World Bank estimates that between 1983 and 2003 about

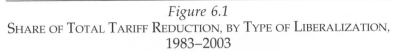

Figure 6.1
SHARE OF TOTAL TARIFF REDUCTION, BY TYPE OF LIBERALIZATION,
1983–2003

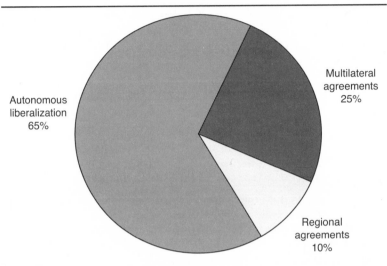

SOURCE: "Regional Trade and Preferential Trading Agreements: A Global Perspective," in *Global Economic Prospects 2005: Trade Regionalism and Development* (Washington, DC: World Bank, 2004), http://siteresources.worldbank.org/INTGEP2005/Resources/GEP107053_h02.pdf.

65 percent of developing-country tariff liberalization (a 21 percent cut in average weighted tariffs) has come about unilaterally, with 25 percent coming from the Uruguay round agreements and only 10 percent from PTAs (Figure 6.1).[4] True, many governments liberalized reluctantly as part of International Monetary Fund and World Bank structural adjustment programs. But the strong and sustained liberalizers have gone ahead under their own steam, without the need for much external pressure. That includes several Latin American countries, eastern Europe, the southeast Asian Tigers, and now China and India.

This brings us to Asia. Modern economic globalization outside the West is an overwhelmingly Asian phenomenon, and much of it is due to unilateral liberalization.

The New Asian Drama and the Chinese Engine[5]

Gunnar Myrdal's *Asian Drama*, written in the 1960s, painted a bleak picture of Asia then and its prospects.[6] This was a continent hobbled by colonial exploitation, trapped in unequal commercial exchange with the West, and mired in myriad market failures that precluded escape from poverty and progress to prosperity. The conclusion that Myrdal and most other development experts drew was that only massive infusions of Western aid, Soviet-style planning, and import-substituting protection could overcome market failures and kick-start industrialization, growth, and development. And in a cultural echo from the same period, V. S. Naipaul dismissed India as a "broken, wounded civilisation." He could have been referring equally to China after the Great Leap Forward and during the Cultural Revolution.

Today these are popular images of Africa, not Asia (at least eastern and southern Asia). How different the Asian Drama looks now— the exact opposite of Myrdal's diagnosis and prognosis. First Japan, South Korea, Taiwan, Hong Kong, and Singapore underwent fast-paced export-oriented industrialization and catch-up growth as a result of stable macroeconomic policies, domestic competition, and opening to the world economy. These policies mattered much more than foreign aid, which, in any case, tapered off from the late 1950s. The southeast Asian Tigers (Malaysia, Thailand, Indonesia, and, to a much lesser extent, the Philippines) followed, with large external opening taking place in the 1980s and the first half of the 1990s. The countries of Indochina, notably Vietnam, started opening their borders as part of their transition from Plan to Market from the mid- to late 1980s.

China started its opening in 1978, with massive trade-and-investment liberalization unleashed from the early 1990s. This was crowned by its accession to the WTO, with by far the strongest commitments of any developing country. India's retreat from the "license raj" began half-heartedly in the 1980s, but a foreign-exchange crisis in 1991 precipitated more radical market-based reforms, including substantial trade and foreign direct investment (FDI) liberalization.

Of course, the story of Asian policy reforms is more complicated. There were lots of factors at play, not least vast differences between countries in historical legacies, policies, and institutions. To varying degrees—and with the exception of free-trade, laissez faire Hong Kong—government intervention, including industrial policies, import protection, and capital controls, coexisted with domestic market-oriented policies and external liberalization. But two big lessons stand out from a half century of policy reforms in first eastern and then southern Asia—what is now "globalizing Asia." First, countries have moved in the direction of the market economy, with better protection of property rights, freer enterprise and competition in place of state ownership and planning, and more exposure to foreign trade and investment. And second, the market economy has opened up personal freedoms and life chances—though not necessarily civic and political freedoms—that were unimaginable even a generation or two ago. That is the product of increasing wealth and the institutions that accompany it.

Now take a closer look at Asia in the world economy, and then at Asian trade-policy reforms.

Asia and Globalization[7]

Asia was conspicuously absent from the world economy from the Industrial Revolution to relatively recent times (though its decline relative to Europe set in well before the Industrial Revolution). This began to change with the post-1950 rise of Japan and the east Asian Tigers, and then changed faster with the opening of first China and then India. The latter two are home to 40 percent of humanity. With still low levels of per capita income (China's being 15 percent, and India's 7 percent, of U.S. levels, measured at purchasing power parity) and huge supplies of cheap, productive labor, they have the potential for stellar catch-up growth rates for decades ahead. Their integration into the world economy, still in its early stages, promises to be more momentous than that of Japan and the east Asian Tigers, and perhaps on a par with the rise of the United States, Germany, and Japan as global economic powers in the late 19th century. (See Figures 6.2 and 6.3, respectively, for changing shares in world gross domestic product [GDP] over time of Asia and of Japan, China, and India.)

Japan still dominates Asian economic activity, accounting for over 50 percent of eastern and southern Asian combined GDP (at market prices). But China is catching up fast. It is already more globally integrated than Japan with regard to trade and FDI penetration and

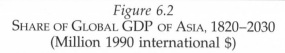

Figure 6.2
SHARE OF GLOBAL GDP OF ASIA, 1820–2030
(Million 1990 international $)

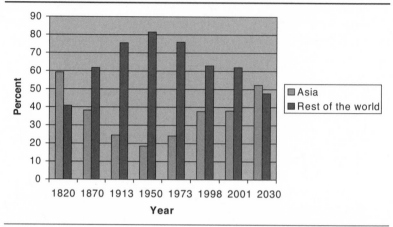

SOURCES: A. Maddison, *Historical Statistics for the World Economy: 1–2003 A.D.*, 2005, http://www.ggdc.net/maddison/Historical_tatistics/horizontal-file_3-2007.xls. For the years 1820–2001, see the sheets World Population, GDP and Per Capita GDP, 1–2003 A.D. in the document. For the year 2030, see A. Maddison, *World Development and Outlook 1830–2030: Evidence submitted to the House of Lords*, Evidence submitted to the Select Committee on Economic Affairs, House of Lords, London, for the inquiry into "Aspects of the Economics of Climate Change," February 20, 2005, http://www.ggdc.net/maddison/.

has recently displaced Japan as the world's third-largest trading nation in goods. China is ranked fourth in the world for trade in services (if intra-EU trade is excluded). By 2005, trade in goods was 63 percent of GDP; FDI annual flows were running at over $70 billion and FDI stock stood at over $300 billion (or about 14 percent of GDP); and multinational enterprises accounted for an astounding 60 percent of merchandise trade (Table 6.1). Thus, the world's most populous nation has, in quick time, mutated from almost complete autarchy to assume the characteristics of a small to medium-sized open economy like South Korea.

India's global integration pales in comparison, but it has come far by its own standards. By 2005, it was the world's 16th-largest trading nation in goods and the 6th largest in services trade. Its share of

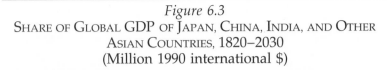

Figure 6.3
SHARE OF GLOBAL GDP OF JAPAN, CHINA, INDIA, AND OTHER
ASIAN COUNTRIES, 1820–2030
(Million 1990 international $)

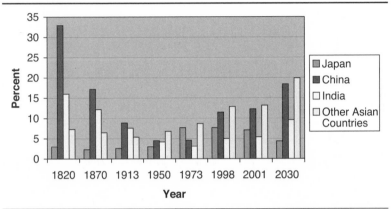

SOURCES: A. Maddison, *Historical Statistics for the World Economy: 1–2003 A.D.*, 2005, http://www.ggdc.net/maddison/Historical_Statistics/horizontal-file_03-2007.xls. For the years 1820–2001, see the sheets World Population, GDP and Per Capita GDP, 1–2003 A.D. in the document. For the year 2030, see A. Maddison, *World Development and Outlook 1830–2030: Evidence submitted to the House of Lords*, Evidence submitted to the Select Committee on Economic Affairs, House of Lords, London, for the inquiry into "Aspects of the Economics of Climate Change," February 20, 2005, http://www.ggdc.net/maddison/.

world trade in goods and services was just under 2 percent, compared with more than 8 percent for China.[8] Trade and FDI stock were 30 percent and 6 percent of GDP, respectively—way below China, but still registering fast growth from a very low base. Annual FDI flows (about $6 billion) and overall FDI stock (just more than $30 billion) were under a 10th of Chinese levels (Table 6.1). Other south Asian countries have also seen global integration and economic progress, but this has been hampered by severe political instability and ethnic strife.

Finally, countries in southeast Asia are highly dependent on the world economy. Like China, FDI-driven exports are central to their growth models. Southeast Asian trade levels are now lower than China's, which represents rapid Chinese trade growth and catch-up

Table 6.1
Economic and Trade Indicators of Asian Countries, 2005

Country	GDP (US$ billion)	GDP growth (%)	Population (million)	Per capita GDP (US$)	PPP GDP (US$ billion)	Merchandise exports (US$ billion)	Service exports (US$ billion)	Total merchandise trade (US$ billion)	Services trade (US$ billion)	Ratio of trade to GDP (%)	FDI inflow (US$ billion)	FDI inward stock/ GDP (%)
China	2,228.9	9.9	1,304.5	1,708.6	8,572.7	761.9	73.9	1,422.0	157.1	63.8	72.4	14.3
Indonesia	287.2	5.6	220.6	1,302.2	847.4	86.2	5.1	155.7	22.3	54.2	5.3	7.4
Malaysia	130.1	5.3	25.3	5,134.4	274.8	140.9	18.95	255.6	40.5	196.5	4.0	36.7
Philippines	98.3	5.1	83.1	1,183.6	408.6	41.3	4.5	88.7	10.3	99.2	1.1	14.3
Singapore	116.8	6.4	4.4	26,836.1	130.2	229.6	45.1	429.7	89.1	367.9	20.1	160.1
Thailand	176.6	4.5	64.2	2,749.4	549.3	110.1	20.5	228.3	48.0	129.3	3.7	32.0
Vietnam	52.4	8.4	83.0	631.7	254.0	31.6	3.9	68.1	8.6	130.0	2.0	59.4
ASEAN-6	861.4	5.9	480.6	1,792.3	2,464.3	639.7	98.05	1,226.1	218.8	142.3	36.2	41.5
India	785.5	8.5	1094.6	717.6	3,815.5	95.1	56.1	229.9	108.3	29.3	6.6	5.8
Japan	4,505.9	2.7	128.0	35,214.5	3,943.7	595.0	107.9	1,109.8	240.5	24.6	2.8	2.2
South Korea	787.6	4.0	48.3	16,309.0	1,056.1	284.4	43.9	545.7	101.7	69.3	7.2	8.0
Taipei	346.4	4.1	22.7	15,291.8	—	197.8	25.6	380.3	57.1	109.8	1.6*	12.1*
Hong Kong	177.7	7.3	6.9	25,593.6	214.5	292.1	62.2	592.3	94.6	333.3	35.9	299.9
TOTAL	9,693.4	—	3,085.6	3,141.5	20,066.8	2,866.0	467.65	5,506.1	978.1	—	162.7	—
World	44,384.9	4.0	6,437.8	6,894.4	61,006.6	10,392.5	2,452.0	21,045.1	4,827.3	47.4	916.3	22.8*

*Whole of Taiwan

Sources: For GDP, population, per capita GDP, merchandise exports, service exports, total merchandise trade, and service trade, "WTO Statistics Database," http://stat.wto.org/Home/WSDBHome.aspx?Language=; for GDP growth, World Bank, "Key Development Data & Statistics" http://web.worldbank.org/WBSITE/EXTERNAL/DATASTATISTICS/0,,contentMDK:20535285~menuPK:1192694~pagePK:64133150~piPK:64133175~theSitePK:239419,00.html; for FDI inflows and FDI inward stock, UNCTAD FDI statistics website, http://www.unctad.org/Templates/Page.asp?intItemID=3198&lang=1. World figures were collected from World Bank, Development Indicators database; Taipei GDP growth figures were collected from the Asian Development Bank, "Millennium Development Goals Statistical Tables," http://www.adb.org/Statistics/mdg.asp.

— = Not available: PPP = purchasing power parity; ASEAN = Association of Southeast Asian Nations over the past decade. But they still dwarf Indian trade levels. The average trade-to-GDP ratio in southeast Asia is about 140 percent. FDI inflows (at about $36 billion in 2005) are about half Chinese levels but way ahead of Indian levels (Table 6.1).

What does this tell us about the emerging international and Asian division of labor? Japan, South Korea, Taiwan, Hong Kong, and Singapore have comparative advantage in high-value goods and services. China has clear-cut comparative advantage in labor-intensive manufacturing exports, and increasingly in labor-intensive agricultural exports.

Given its huge pool of cheap labor, India too should be a labor-intensive, FDI-driven exporting powerhouse in industrial goods, as well as a budding exporter of labor-intensive agricultural products. But severe labor-market restrictions strangulate industrial employment. Less than 10 million Indians are employed in the formal manufacturing sector, out of a total employable population of about 500 million. This compares with upward of 150 million Chinese in manufacturing employment. Indian agriculture is hobbled by external and internal trade restrictions—much more so than in China. And the employment-generation effect from services exports is a drop in the ocean compared with what it could be in manufacturing. The much-hyped information technology sector employs only 1 million relatively skilled and educated people.

Southeast Asia in between stands to gain from deeper integration into east Asian manufacturing supply chains, now including China. It is this "Factory Asia" phenomenon (i.e., cross-border networks of "fragmentation-based" trade and investment) that has driven phenomenal growth in trade between China, northeast Asia, and southeast Asia during the past decade. But to exploit these niches fully, the older members of the Association of Southeast Asian Nations must liberalize further, especially in services and agriculture, and strengthen domestic institutions to compensate for their eroded cheap-labor advantage. The newer, poorer ASEAN members should exploit their cheap-labor advantage, especially as relative incomes rise in China. India and the rest of south Asia remain very far from being integrated into east Asian supply chains.

Asia-driven globalization demands massive adjustments. It is triggering mounting protectionist pressures and threatens an anti-globalization backlash. Labor-abundant east and south Asia stand to gain most through fast, catch-up trade and investment-driven growth, which feeds through to poverty reduction and improvement of life chances for the broad majority of people. Developed and other developing countries will gain too through exploitation of their comparative advantages in capital, land, and resource-intensive products. But they will be under increasing pressure in labor-intensive products. This could squeeze not just unskilled and low-skilled workers' real incomes, but also those of the middle classes. Thus, the future holds out the prospect of greater prosperity overall, but perhaps with bigger inequality within and between nations. The political challenge is to keep borders open and extend market-based reforms, while containing inevitable protectionist pressures.

Asian Trade-Policy Reforms

Chapter 3 discussed the global climate for trade policy pre– and post–Asian crisis. Broadly speaking, previous liberalization of trade and FDI has not been reversed, but its forward momentum has slowed. How do east and south Asia fit into this global picture?

Southeast Asia fits the pattern. With the exception of Singapore, government enthusiasm for further liberalization and domestic structural reforms declined markedly during and after the Asian crisis. Overall, southeast Asia presents a varied picture: free-trade Singapore is at one extreme; other old ASEAN members have relatively liberal trade policies (with average tariffs under 10 percent, correspondingly low nontariff barriers [NTBs], and relatively open FDI regimes in manufacturing), but with large pockets of protection in agriculture and services; and the new ASEAN members are still highly protected (Tables 6.2 and 6.3). Of the latter, Vietnam stands out: it has accelerated external liberalization and internal reforms in the run-up to its WTO accession, and is now rapidly integrating into the global economy through FDI-driven exports.[9]

What about China? "Reform" and "Opening" started in 1978, but the whirlwind transformation of China's economy belongs more to the post-Tienanmen phase, especially since 1994. The unification and convertibility of the exchange rate, privatization, the formal recognition of private property rights, and a host of other market-based reforms have followed. Trade liberalization whittled down the protective effect of border NTBs to about 5 percent of imports on the eve of WTO accession in 2001, and the simple average tariff

Table 6.2
BOUND AND APPLIED MFN TARIFFS IN
SELECTED COUNTRIES, 2003–2004

Country	Binding coverage	Bound tariff rate (all goods)	Applied tariff rate (manufactures)	Applied tariff rate (agriculture)	Overall applied tariff
Japan	99.6	5.0	3.3	10.4	4.7
South Korea	94.4	16.1	6.6	42.5	11.9
China	100.0	10.0	9.5	15.0	10.3
Hong Kong	45.7	0.0	0.0	0.0	0.0
Malaysia	83.7	14.5	8.1	2.1	7.3
Thailand	74.7	25.7	14.6	16.2	14.7
Indonesia	96.6	37.1	6.1	8.0	6.4
Philippines	66.8	25.6	6.9	11.8	7.5
Vietnam	—	—	12.9	18.1	13.7
Taiwan	100.0	6.1	5.5	16.3	6.9
Singapore	69.2	6.9	0.0	0.0	0.0
India	73.8	49.8	25.3	30.0	28.3
Pakistan	44.3	52.4	16.1	13.9	15.9
Bangladesh	15.8	163.8	19.2	21.7	19.5
Sri Lanka	37.8	29.8	9.6	15.4	10.2
South Africa	96.5	19.1	5.3	9.1	5.8
Brazil	100.0	31.4	11.0	10.4	10.9
Chile	100.0	25.1	5.9	6.0	5.9
Mexico	100.0	34.9	14.7	26.4	15.9
Australia	97.0	9.9	4.6	1.1	4.2
New Zealand	99.9	10.3	3.4	1.7	3.2

SOURCE: World Bank trade database, http://siteresources.worldbank.org/INTRES/Resources/469232-1107449512766/tar2005a.xls.

NOTE: The figures are simple unweighted averages of the tariff rates in percentages from years 2003 and 2004.
— = Not available.

has come down from 42 percent in 1992 to 16.6. percent in 2001, and then to about 10 percent after WTO accession (Tables 6.2 and 6.3). This brings border barriers down to southeast Asian levels, and well below the developing-country average.

Thus, China undertook enormous trade-and-FDI liberalization, and with it sweeping industrial and agricultural restructuring, in

Table 6.3
COVERAGE RATIO OF NONTARIFF BARRIERS IN IMPORT TRADE*
(UNWEIGHTED, PERCENT), 1984–1993 AND 1997–2000

	1984–87	1988–90	1991–93	1997–2000
China	10.6	23.2	11.3	5.7
Indonesia	94.7	9.4	2.7	3.1
South Korea	8.8	4.0	2.6	1.5
Malaysia	3.7	2.8	2.1	2.3
Philippines	44.9	—	—	1.8
Thailand	12.4	8.5	5.5	2.1

SOURCES: Hoekman et al., (2002, table A-4; WTO, *Trade Policy Review* country reports (various); P. Athukorala et al., "Tariff Reform and the Structure of Protection in Thailand," April 2, 2004, p. 27.
— = Not available.

* Calculated as percentage of import value of HS6 tariff lines affected by NTBs in total imports. NTBs include quantitative restrictions in the form of all types of licenses and import authorization, quotas, import prohibitions, advanced import deposits, foreign exchange restrictions, fixed customs valuations, and state trading monopolies. Figures reported under a given sub-period relates a single year within that sub-period.

the decade *before* WTO accession. Its accession to the WTO, after 14 years of arduous negotiation, locked in these unilateral reforms and took them several steps further.[10] China's WTO commitments are very strong.[11] They exceed those of other developing countries by a wide margin. Indeed, they are almost as strong as the commitments of developed countries; they are much stronger than those of other large developing countries, such as India, Brazil, Egypt, and Nigeria; and they are stronger than those of smaller, open economies in southeast Asia. These comparisons hold not only for tariff ceilings on goods (including agriculture), but also for border and behind-the-border nontariff barriers in goods *and* services. For example, the average import-weighted GATT-bound tariff is 6.8 percent. Trading rights have been fully liberalized; nearly all quotas, licenses, specific tendering arrangements, and price controls have been removed; and there are strong disciplines on state trading enterprises, remaining subsidies, and other NTBs. China has adopted WTO agreements on trade procedures (such as the TRIPS [Trade-Related Aspects of Intellectual Property Rights] and TRIMS [Trade-Related Investment

Measures] agreements) in full and without transition periods. In services, the effect of WTO accession is, roughly, to cut protection by half. This is the most radical services-liberalization program ever seen. Finally, there are detailed commitments on transparency procedures to make sure trade-related laws and regulations are implemented, backed up by administrative and judicial-review procedures to which individuals and firms have recourse. This is nothing short of fundamental legal innovation in China.

Indian trade-policy reforms have not been as dramatic or breathtaking, but are still considerable by Indian standards. In 1991, the average unweighted tariff was 125 percent, with peak tariffs on agricultural products going up to 300 percent. The tariff structure was extremely complicated, and accompanied by extremely high NTBs. Inward investment was either banned or severely restricted. Exchange controls and the internal restrictions of the license raj (almost) completed the picture.

Much has changed 16 years on. Most border NTBs have been removed, as have internal licensing restrictions. Applied tariffs came down to an average of about 28 percent by 2003–04, and further down to about 16 percent by 2005. The maximum tariff on manufactures was progressively lowered to 12.5 percent by 2007. The intention is to bring average tariffs down to ASEAN levels (around 10 percent) soon. Most restrictions on manufacturing FDI have been removed. However, in agriculture, tariffs and NTBs remain much higher (Table 6.3) And severe FDI and domestic regulatory restrictions keep out foreign competition in several big-ticket services sectors.[12]

Since the initial burst in 1991–93, Indian trade and other economic reforms have proceeded in a stop-go manner. They have not been reversed, but they have moved ahead more slowly and fitfully compared with southeast Asia (pre–Asian crisis) and China (pre– and post–Asian crisis). Democratic politics, including the complications of multiparty governing coalitions and the federal division of powers between the coalition Union government and the states, has made faster, more decisive reforms elusive.

Japan, South Korea, and Taiwan are relatively open economies after decades of gradual liberalization, but all three have sent mixed signals on market-based reforms recently. Japan and South Korea have been reluctant to liberalize trade and FDI further (though South

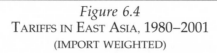

Figure 6.4
TARIFFS IN EAST ASIA, 1980–2001
(IMPORT WEIGHTED)

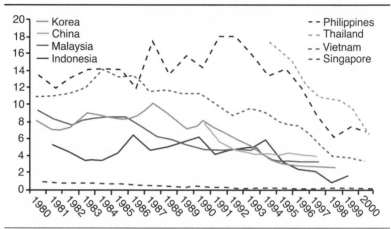

SOURCE: M. Ando and F. Kimura, "The Formation of International Production and Distribution Networks in East Asia," in *International Trade (NBER–East Asia Seminar on Economics)*, vol. 14, ed. T. Ito and A. Rose (Chicago: University of Chicago Press, 2005). First version, NBER Working Paper 10167 (2005), was drawn from Ando and Estevadeordal (2003) (original data source: World Bank Indicators 2002 (CD-ROM)) and also used by Baldwin (2006).

Korea did partially open its financial sector as part of an International Monetary Fund bailout package). Taiwan did liberalize substantially in the run-up to its WTO accession in 2001, though structural reforms have slowed down since.

The reader may wonder how Asia's trade-policy reforms and its global economic integration relate to my emphasis on unilateral liberalization and skepticism regarding trade negotiations. The bottom line is this: first, the northeast and southeast Asian Tigers, and then China and India, have done most of their trade-and-FDI liberalization unilaterally, not through bilateral, regional, or multilateral negotiations.

Nowhere has unilateral liberalization been stronger than in east Asia, especially in the 1980s and 1990s. (See Figure 6.4 for tariff reductions in the region.) In the 1980s, the old ASEAN countries reduced import and inward-investment barriers simultaneously to attract Japanese manufacturing multinational enterprises, which relied on imports of capital goods and components for labor-intensive local processing and assembly of goods for export. This is how they inserted themselves into regional and global manufacturing supply chains, first in electronics and then spreading to other industries (e.g., sport footwear, televisions and radio receivers, office equipment, electrical machinery, power and machine tools, cameras and watches, and printing and publishing). In the 1990s, China also undertook unilateral and simultaneous trade and inward-investment liberalization, and thereby inserted itself as the cheap-labor, final-assembly stage in these expanding supply chains. This in turn triggered additional unilateral liberalization by the southeast Asian countries. More openness to trade and FDI allowed the more advanced ASEAN countries to move up to higher-value production of parts and components in "Factory Asia," while more labor-intensive production migrated to China, and more recently to Vietnam. To repeat, these measures were not brought about by GATT/WTO, ASEAN Free Trade Area, or other free trade agreements (FTAs); rather, they were unilateral responses to market conditions, resulting in market-led regional and global integration.[13]

China's external liberalization now matters most, for it is the biggest the world has ever seen, with the biggest spillover effect in Asia. Most of this was done unilaterally, *before* WTO accession. China's WTO commitments, and its pragmatic, businesslike, and constructive participation in the WTO since accession, are more the consequence than the cause of its sweeping unilateral reforms. Indeed, China is, in many ways, today what Britain was in the second half of the 19th century—the unilateral engine of freer trade. True, China is far from being the top dog Britain was in the 19th century. But it is now the most powerful signal transmitter in the Asian neighborhood. China's opening not only spurred southeast Asian liberalization pre–Asian crisis, but probably helped prevent liberalization reversal post–Asian crisis. It has also encouraged east Asian countries to further liberalize at the margin during the post–Asian crisis—for fear of losing trade and FDI to China. Not least, China has probably had a knock-on effect on India's opening to the world economy. India has recently accelerated its liberalization of tariffs and eased FDI restrictions in some services sectors. This has occurred outside trade negotiations, as was the case with previous Indian trade-and-investment liberalization since 1991. Would this have happened, or happened as fast, if China had not concentrated minds? Probably not.

For other east and south Asian countries to take advantage of the opportunities offered by China's global integration, and overcome more-exposed weaknesses caused by protectionist policies and weak institutions, there has to be further liberalization and regulatory reform. This is less likely to come about through the WTO, PTAs, and regional institutions such as ASEAN and South Asian FTA, and more likely to result from unilateral measures by individual governments in response to internal and external conditions. That is the best prospect for east Asian countries to integrate themselves better into, and reap the benefits from, expanding regional and global supply chains. And that is the best prospect for south Asian countries to insert themselves into these supply chains.

That is not to say that a China-induced unilateral method is a total solution. It is unlikely to induce further external liberalization in the developed world, and least of all in the United States, EU, and Japan. In the developing world, its results will inevitably be patchy and messy. For instance, unilateral liberalization in east Asia, while strong in fragmentation-based manufacturing products that feature in global supply chains, has been weaker in other areas of manufacturing, very uneven in services, and especially weak in agriculture. More generally, unilateral measures do not lock in liberalization against future backtracking. Above all, they do not provide fair, stable, and predictable rules for international commerce. On its own, therefore, unilateral liberalization cannot slay protectionist dragons and solve international commercial conflicts. That leaves room for the WTO and PTAs, but these are, at best, *second* instances of trade policy. The WTO in particular can be a helpful auxiliary, less in driving a future liberalization agenda and more as a set of enforceable nondiscriminatory rules for international commerce, not least to assist developing-country governments in undertaking market-based reforms. But it is important to get priorities right and follow the process bottom up, not top down.

China and the Unilateral Progress to Freer Trade: Post-Doha Priorities

A snapshot of trade policy in Asia today would show the following. As I argued in the last chapter, trade policy across the region looks rather unbalanced. It rests on a shaky PTA leg. Its other WTO leg has gone to sleep; its regional-cooperation arm is limp; and, above all, core abdominal strength through unilateral reforms has weakened after the Asian crisis. China is the conspicuous exception. With the collapse of the Doha round, the Gadarene rush to do more dirty PTAs, and the consequent fraying of the multilateral trading system, three new priorities are called for.

First, China, India, Japan, South Korea, Hong Kong, and the ASEAN countries should be active in plurilateral "coalitions of the willing" to restore the WTO's fortunes, albeit in a sober, realistic manner. This will require U.S. leadership and the cooperation of other major powers. China's helping hand will be indispensable. Once the dust of the Doha round settles, it is vital that China move to the WTO foreground and play an active coleadership role.

Second, there should be much more caution with PTAs. Existing PTAs should be cleaned up and new initiatives launched only with a credible economic strategy. Again, China's lead will be important. It needs to signal its intention to go for strong and clean FTAs, and avoid weak and dirty FTAs. Others will take the hint.

These two points recapitulate what I have said in the previous two chapters. But there is a *third* priority, more important than the other two. It is vital that the Chinese engine of unilateral liberalization does not stall: further global trade-and-FDI liberalization, and related domestic structural reforms, depend on it. Short of a global crisis to concentrate minds, there is no replacement engine for trade-related reforms in Asia and elsewhere.

But this Chinese engine is not preprogrammed. The Beijing leadership is less visionary and more cautious, and domestic protectionist lobbies are more vocal than was the case at the beginning of the decade. Reforms are now in more politically sensitive territory as they bite deeper into domestic regulation and institutions. The momentum for reform continues, but with greater political opposition and at a slower pace. Consequently, the Beijing leadership is likely to go much further with liberalization and structural reforms only if it faces a reasonably clement external macroeconomic and trade environment. This is probably necessary to overcome domestic opposition to change, especially within the Communist Party and the public sector. Tub-thumping protectionism and belligerence by the United States and the EU on the Chinese exchange rate and current-account surplus, garments, and other labor-intensive exports, as well as on security-related issues, will invite a Chinese backlash and make its leadership more defensive. That will likely result in reform slowdown.

Thus, it behooves the United States in the first instance, and then the EU, to strengthen "constructive engagement" with China across a broad range of economic and foreign policy issues, while containing foreign policy hawks and protectionist forces at home. This will, in turn, encourage Beijing to strengthen its key bilateral relationships and its participation in international institutions; contain occasionally aggressive nationalistic tendencies (especially directed at Taiwan and Japan); and, not least, keep up the momentum of economic reforms.[14] Such an alignment will encourage others, such as India, the ASEAN countries, Japan, and South Korea, to act in the same vein. All this is more a matter of unilateral example setting and bilateral cooperation than of trade negotiations.

Conclusion

Largely outside trade negotiations, China is driving Asia's transformation of the world economy. The challenge in China, India, and elsewhere in the developing world is to go further with economic reforms: more trade-and-investment liberalization; much more internal liberalization to integrate the domestic market; and more second-generation institutional reforms to restructure the state so that it supports, not hinders, a complex, globally integrated market economy. The external corollary of economic-policy reforms at home is to anchor constructive engagement abroad and make it permanent, not hostage to the vagaries of a few personalities and stray events.

On that canvas of global politics and economics, the trade-policy challenges of the future will be less amenable to the top-down bureaucratic solutions of the past. Trade-policy reforms will be increasingly of the second-generation variety. They will have to tackle nonborder regulatory barriers that impede trade, foreign investment, and the cross-border movement of workers. These barriers lie deep in domestic policies and institutions. They concern property rights and the legal system, public administration, state-owned

Table 6.4
WORLD RANKING IN EASE OF DOING BUSINESS, 2007

Country	Doing business easily	Starting a business	Dealing with licenses	Employing workers	Registering property	Getting credit	Protecting investors	Paying taxes	Trading across borders	Enforcing contracts	Closing a business
Singapore	1	9	5	1	13	7	2	2	1	4	2
Hong Kong	4	13	60	23	58	2	3	3	3	1	15
Japan	12	44	32	17	48	13	12	105	18	21	1
Thailand	15	36	12	49	20	36	33	89	50	26	44
Malaysia	24	74	105	43	67	3	4	56	21	63	54
South Korea	30	110	22	131	68	36	64	106	13	10	11
Taiwan	50	103	128	148	24	48	64	91	29	92	13
Pakistan	76	59	93	132	88	68	19	146	94	154	51
China	83	135	175	86	29	84	83	168	42	20	57
Vietnam	91	97	63	84	38	48	165	128	63	40	121
Sri Lanka	101	29	160	111	134	97	64	158	60	133	39
Bangladesh	107	92	116	129	171	48	15	81	112	175	102
Philippines	107	92	116	129	171	48	15	81	112	175	102
India	120	111	134	85	112	36	33	165	79	177	137
Indonesia	123	168	99	153	121	68	51	110	41	141	136

SOURCE: World Bank, Doing Business database, www.doingbusiness.org/.

NOTE: The numbers correspond to each country's aggregate ranking on the ease of doing business and on each of the 10 topics that comprise the overall ranking.

Table 6.5
INDICATORS FOR TRADING ACROSS BORDERS, 2007

Country	Ease of trading across borders (world ranking)	Documents for export (number)	Time for export (days)	Cost to export (US$ per container)	Documents for import (number)	Time for import (days)	Cost to import (US$ per container)
Singapore	1	4	5	416	4	3	367
Hong Kong	3	4	6	525	4	5	525
South Korea	13	4	11	745	6	10	745
Japan	18	4	10	989	5	11	1,047
Malaysia	21	7	18	432	7	14	385
Taiwan	29	7	13	747	7	12	747
Indonesia	41	5	21	667	6	27	623
China	42	7	21	390	6	24	430
Thailand	50	7	17	615	9	14	786
Philippines	57	8	17	800	8	18	800
Sri Lanka	60	8	21	810	6	21	844
Vietnam	63	6	24	669	8	23	881
India	79	8	18	820	9	21	910
Pakistan	94	9	24	515	8	19	1,336
Bangladesh	112	7	28	844	9	32	1,148

SOURCE: World Bank, Doing Business database, www.doingbusiness.org/.

NOTE: The costs and procedures involved in importing and exporting a standardized shipment of goods are detailed under this topic. Every official procedure involved is recorded—starting from the final contractual agreement between the two parties and ending with the delivery of the goods.

Table 6.6
PERCENTILE WORLD RANK OF GOVERNANCE INDICATORS FOR ASIAN COUNTRIES, 2006

Country	Voice and accountability	Political stability/ no violence	Government effectiveness	Regulatory quality	Rule of law	Control of corruption
Singapore	46.6	94.7	99.5	99.5	95.2	98.1
Hong Kong	64.9	88.9	93.8	100.0	90.5	92.7
Japan	75.5	85.1	88.2	87.3	90.0	90.3
Malaysia	38.0	58.7	80.6	69.8	65.7	68.0
Taiwan	72.1	63.5	83.9	78.5	74.8	70.4
South Korea	70.7	60.1	82.9	70.7	72.9	64.6
India	58.2	22.1	54.0	48.3	57.1	52.9
Thailand	32.2	16.3	64.9	62.4	55.2	50.5
China	4.8	33.2	55.5	46.3	45.2	37.9
Vietnam	8.2	59.6	41.7	31.2	44.8	29.1
Indonesia	41.3	14.9	40.8	43.4	23.3	23.3
Sri Lanka	36.1	8.2	42.2	50.2	54.3	48.5
Philippines	44.2	11.1	55.0	52.2	41.9	27.2
Bangladesh	30.8	8.7	23.7	20.0	22.9	4.9
Pakistan	12.5	4.8	34.1	38.5	24.3	18.0

SOURCE: World Bank, "Worldwide Governance Indicators: 1996–2006," July 2007, http://web.worldbank.org/WBSITE/EXTERNAL/WBI/EXTWBIGOVANTCOR/0,,contentMDK:20771165~menuPK:1866365~pagePK:6416845~piPK:6416309~theSitePK:1740530,00.html.

NOTE: Percentile rank indicates the percentage of countries worldwide that rate below the country (subject to margin of error). Higher values indicate better governance ratings. Percentile ranks have been adjusted to account for changes over time in the set of countries covered by the governance indicators.

enterprises, capital markets, labor markets, services regulation, intellectual property, competition and investment rules, customs administration, public procurement, product standards, corporate law and bankruptcy procedures, and other issues besides. Related reforms are technically complicated, locally specific, administratively demanding, and politically very sensitive. They are bundled with domestic politics and economics; initiating and implementing them are overwhelmingly a domestic affair; and the scope for productive international negotiations and solutions is restricted. And it is precisely in all these areas that China and India still do very badly— as the World Bank's business-climate and governance indicators show. (See Tables 6.4 and 6.5 on red tape barriers to business, trade, and governance in Asian countries, and Table 6.6 on governance indicators in Asian countries.)

To sum up, freer trade in the early 21st century, and modern globalization more generally, are happening more "from below" than "from above." Their engine, now to be found in Asia, particularly in China, is bottom-up liberalization and regulatory reform that spread through competitive emulation, like ripples and waves across seas and oceans. This process is not driven by international institutions. As the German economist Wilhelm Röpke noted, "Internationalism, like charity, begins at home"; it emerges "from within and beneath"; like a house, it cannot be built "starting with the roof"; and "more important than international institutions and legal constructions are the moral-political forces behind the market that are only really effective within nations."[15]

7. Conclusion: The Future of Free Trade

Beginning with David Hume and Adam Smith, the emphasis on free trade has been not just one of the postulates, but the very heart or essence, of economic liberalism.

—Jan Tumlir

In political activity, then, men sail a boundless and bottomless sea; there is neither harbour for shelter nor floor for anchorage, neither starting point nor appointed destination. The enterprise is to keep afloat on an even keel; the sea is both friend and enemy; and the seamanship consists in using resources of a traditional manner of behaviour to make a friend of every hostile occasion.

—Michael Oakeshott

This book has taken stock of trade policy in the early 21st century. It began with an intellectual history of free trade versus protection; then surveyed the political economy of trade-policy reform, especially in developing countries; then moved to the World Trade Organization, preferential trade agreements (PTAs), unilateral liberalization, and the rise of Asia. Now, in closing, I shift from the present to the future of trade policy. What are the real-world prospects for free (or freer) trade in the years and decades ahead? How will it fare against existing and emerging protectionist threats? And how can one best make the case for free trade in the future?

Optimists will look forward to further advances for free trade in globalization's wake. But others will be more pessimistic, or at least sound a cautionary note. Protectionism, they would say, lurks everywhere. It is safe to say that protectionism will still be around in midcentury, and the battle between it and free trade will continue to rage. That is one clear lesson from economic history and the history of ideas.

The quotes above hint at the balance I seek. They juxtapose the classical-liberal free-trade ideals of Jan Tumlir with the pragmatism expressed in one of Michael Oakeshott's most quoted passages. Free trade is a desirable goal, and progress in that direction, however gradual and piecemeal, should be integral to modern globalization. But politics is a practical, messy affair. To borrow Oakeshott's seafaring metaphor, the ship of state has trouble enough staying afloat on an even keel in turbulent seas. Sensible political economy has to factor this in. That is what I have tried to do in the previous chapters. The question now is how it applies to the future of free trade.

The first sections of this chapter review free trade today, in theory and in practice. The following sections look ahead. What are the emerging facts on the ground with regard to global political and economic trends? And what of the case for free trade in the future?

Taking Stock: The Case for Free Trade, Past and Present

Chapter 2 summarized the main political and economic arguments in favor of free trade. To recapitulate, metaeconomic arguments for free trade date back at least two millennia. An intellectual tradition from early Christian thought to Richard Cobden, Woodrow Wilson, and Cordell Hull holds that open and flourishing international commerce brings about better understanding between peoples and buttresses peaceful, ever-closer international relations.

The *economic* case for free trade emerged one-and-a-half millennia later. Adam Smith's genius was to draw on preexisting traditions of moral philosophy and economics to lay out a system of interrelating economic phenomena animated by laissez faire, what he called "natural liberty." This he extended to international trade.

Smith's system has been refined down the past two centuries. An international division of labor according to comparative advantage allocates resources more efficiently, resulting in the greater wealth of nations. It integrates hitherto separated national economies into a worldwide *cooperative* system that caters for reciprocal wants. There are all-around material gains, for rich and poor countries alike.

These are the short-term (or static) gains from trade. That is but the necessary preface for capital accumulation, economies of scale, and other long-run (or dynamic) gains, such as the transfer of technology and skills, and the competitive spur that comes from exposure to world-class standards of practice. This feeds into productivity gains, increases in real incomes, and economic growth. Indeed, it is the dynamic gains from trade that Smith and his contemporary

David Hume emphasized. They strongly linked free trade (broadly defined to include cross-border flows of capital and people) to domestic institutions and growth, all on the canvas of the long-run progress of commercial society.

Adam Smith fortified his presumption in favor of free trade with an explicit political argument. Protectionism is driven by "the clamorous importunity of partial interests" that capture government and prevent it from having "an extensive view of the general good." Free trade, in contrast, tilts the balance away from rent-seeking producer interests and toward the mass of consumers. It is part of a wider constitutional package to keep government limited, transparent, and clean, enabling it to concentrate better on the public good.

As important to Smith and Hume was the *moral* case for free trade, centered on individual freedom. Individual choice is the engine of free trade, and of progressive commercial society more generally. It sparks what Hume called a "spirit of industry"; it results in much better life chances, not just for the select few but for individuals in the broad mass of society who are able to lead more varied and interesting lives.

To sum up, free trade is of course associated with standard economic efficiency arguments. But the classical-liberal case for free trade is more rounded, taking in the moral imperative of individual freedom and linking it to prosperity. Finally, free trade contributes to, though it does not guarantee, peaceful international relations. Freedom, prosperity, security: this trinity lies at the heart of the case for free trade.

Taking Stock: Free Trade in Practice

Chapter 3 argued that the historical record shows that countries that are more open to the world economy perform better than those that are less open or remain closed. This of course runs counter to the assertions of liberalization-and-globalization skeptics.

External trade has been a "handmaiden" of growth since classical antiquity.[1] Trade across frontiers promoted "Smithian" growth (real-income gains from the integration of geographically separated markets) in ancient Greece and Rome, during the Sung period in China, at the time of the Mauryas in India and the Abbasids in the Middle

117

East, and in the Europe of the Middle Ages. Smithian growth continues apace in developed and developing countries. Since the Industrial Revolution, it has been supplemented by the "Promethean" growth powered by successive technological revolutions.[2]

The evidence of the past two centuries, roughly since the post-Napoleonic settlement, supports the proposition that economies grow faster and get richer the more open they become. One of Lord Bauer's chief insights was that economic advancement in the developing world has occurred in countries and regions that have had the most contact with the outside world, and particularly with the advanced centers of the world economy in the West. Indeed, no country on Earth has seen a sustained rise in living standards without being open to the world.[3]

The more detailed evidence, post-1945, points in the same direction. The gradual liberalization of trade and capital flows in the Organisation for Economic Co-operation and Development spurred west European reconstruction, recovery, and catch-up growth. The outward orientation of Japan and other east Asian countries played an important role in their catch-up growth. The massive liberalization of foreign trade and inward investment in China, in tandem with internal liberalization, has contributed to spectacular and sustained growth since the 1980s. Similar forces have been at work in India since the 1990s. Hence, liberalization of trade and foreign direct investment (FDI) is central to Asia's unfolding transformation of the global economy. Strong liberalizers elsewhere have also reaped growth and welfare gains, notably east European countries, Chile, Australia, and New Zealand.

Such is the good news for the bulk of the world's population that live in the Organisation for Economic Co-operation and Development countries, plus about 25 "new-globalizing" developing countries. The bad news is that this leaves about 1.5 billion people in over 50 less globalized, worse-performing countries. These are low-income and least-developed countries that have liberalized less, though they suffer too from other intractable problems, such as poor climate and geography, rampant disease, ethnic conflict, civil war, and chronically corrupt and predatory governments.

External liberalization, it must be emphasized, is not a panacea. Questions of how it is sequenced with other economic and political reforms, and whether it should proceed fast or slow, will find different answers in different countries at different times. Furthermore, trade liberalization on its own may not deliver much. But *in interaction with* market-friendly domestic policies and institutions, there are abundant, long-term gains to be had. External opening creates the spontaneous stimulus for institutional upgrading to better exploit trade and investment opportunities, for example, through better currency and banking practices and the development of ports and inland communications. Reciprocally, the gains for importers, exporters, and domestic and foreign investors are maximized by better enforcement of property rights and contracts; cleaner, more efficient public administration; and simpler, more transparent regulations for doing business; as well as more investment in infrastructure. Openness, to repeat, is a *handmaiden* of growth, not a quick fix.

What of the policy framework to support a freer-trading system? This was the subject of Chapters 4–6.

A workable WTO, focused on market access and supporting nondiscriminatory rules, is important. But the WTO has not delivered, especially in the Doha round. It is going to be very difficult to put the WTO on the right track. To do so, more modesty and realism are in order. The WTO is unlikely to deliver further substantial multilateral liberalization. The best that can be hoped for is modest, incremental multilateral liberalization where feasible. More important will be a stronger focus on safeguarding and improving vital multilateral trade rules.

PTAs are no substitute for a workable WTO. In certain conditions, they can reinforce market reforms, but only if they are strong, comprehensive, WTO-plus, competition-enhancing agreements. Nearly all PTAs, though, are weak, trade-light, and full of discriminatory provisions that potentially restrict trade—more fluffy foreign policy than commercially sensible arrangements. That is the emerging reality in Asia-Pacific, reflecting what has happened already in other developing-country regions. Although today's PTAs do not presage a breakdown in the world trading system, their rampant discrimination is creating worrying political and economic complications.

That leaves the unilateral method as the driving force of external liberalization in the developing world. Trade negotiations and agreements have their place, but unilateral liberalization comes first. Now its engine is China. That, more than trade negotiations, is and will be the spur to further trade and FDI liberalization elsewhere in Asia and beyond. It is vital that China continue with trade and related domestic reforms. That depends on a host of internal and external political and economic conditions.

Looking Ahead: World Political-Economic Trends

As argued in Chapter 6, the new Asian Drama, particularly the opening of first China and then India, is a defining feature of early 21st-century globalization. Developing Asia's transformation of the world economy, still in its early stages, promises to be as momentous as the entry of the United States, Germany, and Japan into the world economy in the last third of the 19th century. It could even herald the biggest global economic transformation since the Industrial Revolution. These effects will unfold over the course of the next few decades. What are the implications?

Emerging trends show that the classical argument for free trade is as relevant as ever. Trade and related economic reforms enable China, India, and other Asian countries to better exploit their comparative advantages in a more specialized international division of labor. Market-based reforms also provide the stimulus for inward investment; the transfer of technology and skills; and a more competitive, entrepreneurial business environment. These replenishing gains boost growth, which in turn leads to poverty reduction.

The rest of the world gains too. Consumers elsewhere can buy cheaper and more varied products. Developed-country firms cater to expanding Chinese and Indian demand for capital- and skill-intensive inputs to local production, as well as for finished goods and services. By "offshoring" low-value manufacturing and services activities, these firms can scale up, improve productivity, and generate better-skilled, higher-paying jobs at home. Exporters in resource-abundant developed and developing countries are also discovering large new markets for commodities—witness China's voracious appetite for oil, gas, minerals, metals, and agricultural commodities.

That said, these all-around comparative advantage–based gains mask tensions and potential conflict. The effective doubling to quadrupling of the world's workforce since 1980—very much the result of China's and India's insertion into the world economy—has shifted the relationship between global capital and labor. Labor-intensive exports from Asia are displacing cheap-labor activities while increasing returns to capital- and knowledge-intensive activities in the West.

As more tasks are "unbundled" and offshored to developing countries, there is more pressure on midskilled activities performed by middle-class workers in the West. The net result is widening inequality, possibly now extending to middle-class incomes. The magnitude of these effects is still unclear, and perhaps prone to exaggeration. But the potential for them to bite deeper is evident, especially with more intensive North-South trade.[4]

Many developing countries without abundant natural resources also face a stiffer competitive challenge. This applies in particular to countries with labor-intensive manufacturing activities squeezed by Chinese competition and caught in a "middle-income trap."[5]

The danger is that wider inequality and a middle-class squeeze in the West, combined with the squeeze on developing countries caught in a middle-income trap, will undermine support for globalization and lead to a protectionist backlash. This will be directed at China in the first instance, but also at India. This threatens to slow down globalization and diminish its benefits—not just for developing countries with huge numbers of poor people, but also for the vast middle classes in the developed world.

What is to be done? Luddite protectionism, either in the West or in the developing world, is not the answer. It will benefit a minority of cosseted, politically well-connected producers and other rent seekers at the expense of everyone else.

A seemingly more reasonable alternative is what could be labeled "globalization and social democracy." This world view is increasingly popular in policy-wonking circles in Europe and North America. It holds that borders must be kept open so that globalization can deliver its benefits. But, within the border, governments should have an expansive, interventionist, redistributive role. This entails making taxation more progressive; supporting social safety nets; targeting assistance at workers who lose their jobs as a result of imports; and providing infrastructure and public services such as health care, education, and training. Active, enabling government is needed to "compensate losers," shore up domestic support for globalization, and adapt economies to global competition.[6]

In essence, globalization and social democracy is an update of the post-1945 Bretton Woods compromise (otherwise known as "Smith abroad and Keynes at home," or more clumsily as "the compromise of embedded liberalism"). It also dovetails with the postwar theory of commercial policy, which holds that free trade abroad is compatible with government intervention to remedy domestic market failures (as outlined in Chapter 2).

The first part of the equation is correct: borders must be kept open so that globalization can continue apace. And yes, this does require domestic political management to prevent a protectionist backlash. But the second, "social-democratic" part of the equation is, in my view, incorrect. Governments do have a role to provide public goods, such as basic social safety nets, education, health care, and infrastructure. But this does not necessitate open-ended intervention. There is, after all, a long record of "government failure" in these areas, in the West as well as in the Rest. Indeed, government failure is as prevalent at home as it is when governments interfere with international commerce. Overactive government rigidifies domestic labor markets and other aspects of economic activity—at a time when more, not less, flexibility is required so that national economies can adapt effectively to keener global competition.

Hence, classical liberals would make a strong case for *limited* government at home as well as abroad, and for free trade (or laissez faire) at home as well as abroad. Limited government—not to be confused with minimal government or a "night watchman state"[7]— would eschew higher levels of taxation and complicated labor-market interventions. It would encourage, not discourage, competition among private-sector providers of infrastructure, health, education, and training services. This should include opening up these sectors to international competition. Such measures would run with, not against, the grain of globalization, which is blurring the divide between international and domestic activities by making swathes of the latter more tradable. That includes public services traditionally run along command-economy lines.

My view is that a classical-liberal frame of limited government and free trade is better suited to adapting national economies to globalization than the schizophrenia of globalization and social democracy. In addition to underestimating government failure, the latter has different and contradictory sets of tools for the international and domestic spheres, premised on an increasingly untenable divide between what is "international" and what is "domestic." Classical liberalism, in contrast, has complementary, market-based sets of tools for international and domestic policies, and makes no artificial distinction between the two spheres.

In addition to the new Asian Drama, there are other emerging global political-economic trends that will likely move center stage in the years and decades to come. To highlight several:

First, the freedom of people to move hither and yon in search of work was part of 19th-century free trade in practice. This was reversed in the 20th century. Like freeing up the international exchange of goods and services and capital mobility, loosening pervasive restrictions on cross-border labor movement promises large gains for developing and developed countries. It helps to plug labor shortages in rich countries with aging and shrinking populations, and with relatively affluent people unwilling to do low-paying menial work. It provides an outlet for people in poor countries in search of a better life. In turn, they remit large sums of money to families back home. If the incentives are right, many will return to their homelands with capital, skills, and contacts to world markets. Generally, hard-working migrants and temporary foreign workers inject energy and vitality into often complacent, decadent, and vegetative societies.[8]

Still, a note of political and social realism is in order. Opening borders to people is much more sensitive than opening borders to trade and capital flows. International trade takes place "in the company of strangers." FDI is closer to home, but having foreigners as one's coworkers and neighbors is really up close.[9] There are legitimate concerns about assimilating people from very different cultures into liberal societies while preserving the rule of law and social stability. And there are understandable anxieties about an excessive "multiculturalism" that tolerates foreign religious and other extremists who propagate intolerance and violence.

None of these concerns should detract from the basic case for more open borders for the movement of people. But they do argue in favor of a cautious, gradual, and controlled process—a long-term project akin to the half century it took to liberalize tariffs under the General Agreement on Tariffs and Trade. This demands political patience and resourcefulness. Nevertheless, it should be at the heart of a 21st-century free-trade agenda.

Second, inter-developing-country trade—already 40 percent of their overall trade—is throttled by the high barriers developing countries erect against one another. Significant developing-country liberalization would not only improve own productivity, but would also allow low-income and least-developed countries to better exploit their comparative advantages by exporting to middle-income developing countries, as well as to the fast-growing markets of China and India. It is incumbent on major regional powers, notably China, India, Brazil, and South Africa, to unilaterally open their markets. That, more than the WTO and PTAs, would enable often-blighted neighboring countries to share in their growth and prosperity. It would also contribute to regional peace and stability.

Third, many developing countries are mired in wretched poverty, disease, crime, and murderous internal strife. States are failing miserably or have collapsed. This affects much of Africa, but it is not restricted to Africa. Paul Collier estimates that close to one billion people—the "bottom billion"—live in almost 60 such states.[10] The old solutions of aid and policy driven by international organizations have not worked. Grandiose blueprints for significantly more aid are highly unlikely to work. Nor is seemingly more modest World Bank thinking that better-performing states should be rewarded with more and better-targeted aid. All such ideas are suffused with misguided top-down planning, political naivety, and the self-serving interests of those in the aid business. But that still leaves failed and failing states with venal and thuggish ruling elites, and without the history and institutions to sustain market-based reforms "from below." The dilemma is real; problems may get worse; and they will spill over into luckier parts of the world in the form of refugees, illegal migrants, and terrorism.

Fourth, the "low politics" of trade and related economic policies cannot be divorced from the "high politics" of international security (or the lack of it). There are new global security flashpoints post–cold war and post–September 11: Islamic fundamentalism and the international terror networks fanning out from the oil-rich Middle East; military rivalry between established and rising powers, especially between the United States and China; and the scramble for energy resources, also involving competition among the powers. All threaten the free movement of people, goods, and services across land, seas, and skies. It is all too tempting to use "national security" as a cloak for protectionism. This has to be contained, and a sensible balance found between legitimate security goals and unfettered international commerce.

Fifth, investment nationalism is on the rise, and it is often twinned with energy nationalism. State-owned or state-linked energy companies from China, India, and Russia are aggressively chasing markets and securing supplies abroad, aided and abetted by home-government industrial policy. There are more examples of Organisation for Economic Co-operation and Development and developing-country governments discriminating against foreign investors to protect "national champions."

FDI is critically important to developed countries and new-globalizing developing countries. There are now emerging multinationals from China, India, and other developing countries. Hence, there is an overriding general interest to prevent investment nationalism from getting out of hand and to have simple, transparent, and predictable rules to guarantee the freedom to invest abroad.

Sixth, the clamor to combat global warming risks becoming the new Trojan horse for protectionism. There may be a case for taking precautionary measures to deal with the threats posed by climate change, and these measures will require action at regional and global levels. But the climate-change debate is already full of hot air—"all fart and no shit," as my father used to say. The atmosphere is befogged with puffy ideas to subsidize this or that initiative and tax this or that "environmental bad." Climate change has rapidly become a lightning-rod issue for ad hoc, bureaucratic, costly interventions, and it could easily spill over into protection against imports. There is a wrong way to link trade policy to climate change. The right way is to take economically efficient precautionary measures (such as a simple carbon tax) while keeping borders open to international commerce.

Seventh, "standards protectionism" is an established feature of trade policy. Onerous technical, food-safety, intellectual property, labor, and environmental standards are aimed at restricting mainly labor-intensive exports from developing countries. The pressure for greater "standards harmonization" can only increase, and with it comes what Jagdish Bhagwati calls "regulatory intrusionism" that undermines developing countries' cost advantages.[11]

Product and other standards directly imposed by governments are not the only threat, however. The last decade has seen the rise of voluntarily agreed global standards on all manner of commercial activities, usually in the name of "corporate social responsibility" and involving the cooperation of governments, multinational firms, nongovernmental organizations (NGOs), and international organizations. So far, the bulk of these standards have been of the "soft" variety, without the sanction of national or international law. But there is pressure to make them "harder" and more coercive, with government backing and legal sanction. This would widen the range of regulatory intrusionism and backdoor protectionism aimed at developing countries. Huge multinational firms may manage comfortably in this kind of world, but it threatens to restrict profitable commercial opportunities for smaller firms employing mostly poor workers. They are less able to bear the costs involved. That is the real danger of direct and indirect standards protectionism.[12]

Protectionist viruses need carriers. Organized rent-seeking interests that benefit directly from protectionism are longstanding carriers. Business groups and unionized labor in cahoots with politicians and bureaucrats are familiar culprits. But they would not be effective without powerful ideological opposition to free trade. The latter has changed form since the collapse of communism and the end of the cold war. The *sentimental*, postcommunist and postmodern opposition to globalization, and markets generally, is now led by a congeries of NGOs.

Globalization, then, faces the opposition of an alliance, witting or not, between old-style rent-seeking interests and new-style ideological forces. One is reminded of John Stuart Mill's reference to "the numerous sentimental enemies of political economy, and its still more numerous interested enemies in sentimental guise."[13] Militant anti-globalization activists are bit-part players in the opposition. More important are establishment figures—senior politicians, leading officials in international organizations and in NGOs, prominent CEOs, distinguished journalists, and academics. They are what David Henderson calls "New Millennium Collectivists" who push for soft and hard interventions in the world economy. They will be a formidable threat to free trade in decades to come.

Looking Ahead: Making the Case for Free Trade in the New Century

The core political and economic case for free trade, in the service of the trinity of freedom, prosperity, and security, is as relevant as ever in the early 21st century. It will be as relevant in the decades ahead. The point is to update and adapt it to keep up with ever-changing realities—not least to meet the emerging global challenges described above. How must it adapt?

First, the post-1945 case for free trade, based on the Bretton Woods compromise and the postwar theory of commercial policy, is too narrow and mechanical. Free trade should burst these chains and return to its classical-liberal foundations in Smith and Hume.

As outlined in Chapter 2, the Bretton Woods and GATT settlements combined a partial restoration of 19th-century free trade with expanding government intervention at home. Postwar trade theory reflected such "mixed-systems thinking" by decoupling free trade from laissez faire. In addition, "liberalism from above" has prevailed: trade liberalization has relied on international organizations and intergovernmental negotiations.

Both mixed-systems thinking and liberalism from above were politically expedient after World War II, but over time, they have entrenched misguided conventional wisdoms. The first is that Big Government interventionism at home will not flood across borders and overly damage international commerce. The second is that international institutions deliver trade liberalization "from outside," and only through "concessions" to foreigners in a game of haggling. On both counts, New Millennium Collectivists and even supposedly globalization-friendly social democrats believe that governments have the knowledge, capacity, and honesty to remedy domestic and international market failures. They persistently underestimate government failure, both at home and abroad.

Mixed-systems thinking forgets that free trade is part and parcel of free markets; it is but an element of a constitutional whole that includes limited government and laissez faire at home. Of course, there can be no exact return to mid-Victorian British conditions, especially in conditions of modern democratic politics. But free trade should be *recoupled* to laissez faire, within a framework of rules enforced by limited—but not minimalist—government.

From Hume and Smith to Hayek, the classical-liberal approach to economic order has been to stress the need for general rules of conduct in a more complex world. As the world becomes more complex in globalization's wake, it does not follow that government activity should become more complex too. In an ever-extending global market economy, governments simply lack the detailed knowledge to make selective interventions work. In Hayek's words, they are "constitutionally ignorant." Ratcheting up the output of detailed regulations is not the answer. On the contrary, *simplicity* is the key. Rather than intervening left, right, and center in the economic *process*, governments should concentrate on regulating the overall economic *order*, that is, the "framework conditions" of economic activity.[14] To Michael Oakeshott, this requires governments to be "umpires" of "civic associations," not "estate managers" of "enterprise associations."[15] Umpiring consists of setting and enforcing general rules of conduct for the economic order as a whole. Estate managing, in contrast, caters to a superabundance of rent-seeking interests.

General rules of conduct are simple, transparent, nondiscriminatory, and *negative*: they tell actors what not to do, but otherwise leave them free to do as they wish. They are generally proscriptive, not prescriptive. Applying equally to all, they exist to protect private property rights and contracts in defense of individual freedom, and as the basis for entrepreneurship and growth. They are intended to *limit* government, not extend its regulatory reach. Within national jurisdictions, these rules are embodied in private (or commercial) law, the legal underbelly of market society. Domestic private law has its external complements in international private law and in aspects of international public law that govern cross-border commerce, especially the most favored nation and national treatment clauses of the GATT. The latter enjoin governments *not* to discriminate in international trade. Their effect is to help defend private property rights against big, discretionary government in international transactions.[16]

In essence, classical liberalism, unlike social democracy, emphasizes complementary and joined-up approaches to domestic and international economic order. Limited government and laissez faire at home underpin limited government and free trade abroad, and domestic rules should be similar to international rules.

What about liberalism from above? My view (as set out in Chapter 6) is that 21st-century free trade should rely less on 20th-century liberalism from above and more on 19th-century liberalism from below. With the latter method, the liberalization impulse comes from national governments acting unilaterally (or autonomously), and spreads internationally by example (or competitive emulation).

Unilateral free trade makes economic sense, since welfare gains come quicker from own, unconditional import liberalization than from protracted international negotiations. It makes political sense too. Governments have the flexibility to initiate policies and emulate better practice abroad in experimental, trial-and-error fashion, tailored to specific local conditions. The WTO and bilateral and regional trade agreements can be helpful auxiliaries in advancing a liberalization agenda, but they are poor substitutes to unilateral, bottom-up liberalization.

Second, national governance is as crucial as ever. This statement contradicts the shibboleths of "global governance." Votaries of the latter say that the nation-state is in retreat before the advancing battalions of globalization. National governments, acting separately and independently, are unable to cope with global problems, such as pollution, disease, job losses, and health, education, and gender issues. The core prescription follows: "global governance" should provide "global solutions" to tackle "global problems." Global governance should involve partnerships of governments, international organizations, NGOs, big business, and organized labor, acting in concert across a wide range of public policies.[17]

This worldview is utterly distorted. In all developed countries, and in most developing countries, national governments, not NGOs, provide core functions of law and public policy. These functions of national governance—defense of territory from external threat, political stability and internal law and order, the protection of property rights, the provision of macroeconomic stability and other public goods—are as vital as ever. Governments still set the policy stance on international trade, FDI, portfolio capital flows, and the cross-border movement of people. National policy, much more than any instrument of global governance, shapes national institutions. It is this combination of national policies and institutions that largely determines national integration with the global economy and national economic performance.[18]

Right through the 19th century, national governance, in the context of a decentralized system of nation-states, coexisted with increasing international economic integration. Has the globalization-and-governance equation changed so much over a century later? Arguably not. Globalization continues to depend fundamentally on law-governed nation-states. Put another way, the preconditions of a good or bad, healthy or sick, liberal or illiberal international economic order are to be found "within and beneath," as Wilhelm Röpke put it—in the subsoil of nation-states.

This is not to deny the importance of international cooperation where national-level action is insufficient. Even a skeptic of global governance may concede that there are legitimate zones of international cooperation, and that more of it is required now compared with the 19th century. However, good policy demands a clear specification of problems and, if concerted action is necessary, a sense of the extent and limits of such action. Multilateralism works when it has easy-to-grasp, limited, realistic means and ends. That is an argument for caution and modesty. Unfortunately, the post-1945 record of most international institutions has been one of hubristic ambition, empty rhetoric, diffuse and mutually contradictory objectives, dysfunctional bureaucracy, and indeed corruption. It has mostly exacerbated misguided government intervention at home. The aid business is a case in point. The GATT was a notable exception, but the same cannot be said of the WTO. To cap it all, the global-governance catchphrase—"global solutions for global problems"—assumes, wrongly, that most problems have to be dealt with by—usually unaccountable, unrepresentative, and distant—members of the "international community." It is this unconditional embrace of global governance that is glib, illiberal, and dangerous.

Third, trade policy must work with the grain of wider geopolitical realities. This book has placed trade policy in the frame of economic policy, and it has stressed the primacy of national economic policies and institutions. But trade policy also links up to foreign policy and international politics, for this frame is also indispensable. A reasonably stable international political order is the categorical imperative for economic development. Without the global Pax—an orderly framework for international relations—there can be no security for national and international commerce.

Geopolitical realities have changed since the end of the cold war. No serious challenge exists to U.S. leadership abroad after the collapse of the Soviet Imperium. Europe and Japan are internally sclerotic and externally pusillanimous. Long-term demographic trends, with aging and shrinking populations, make European and Japanese leadership prospects bleaker. Other powers are on the rise, notably China and India. The transatlantic alliance, while still important, is no longer the fulcrum of international relations. Politics and economics are shifting inexorably in an Asia-Pacific direction. Finally, there are new security challenges, especially after September 11.

The one constant in this shifting political template is U.S. leadership. For the foreseeable future, the United States will remain the indispensable anchor for global security, prosperity, and freedom— far more important than any international organization or international treaty. It is vital that the United States leads from the front in securing the global Pax against systemic threats; in dealing with failed states; in maintaining open and stable international financial markets; and, not least, in containing protectionism and encouraging the further liberalization of trade, capital flows, and the movement of people around the world. The United States must also lead by example, setting the standard for liberal economic policies worldwide by what it does at home. This includes untying existing knots of domestic protectionism.

U.S. leadership has to be exercised on several tracks: unilaterally; bilaterally and regionally, especially in relations with other powers; and multilaterally through international institutions. Daunting domestic and external obstacles stand in the way of the enlightened exercise of U.S. power and influence abroad. Domestic politics is shot through with parochialism, protectionism, and short-termism, all of which increasingly hamper the exercise of a credible, long-term, outward-looking foreign policy. Externally, the United States has been overideological, unempirical, and ham-fisted in its dealings with other powers and in international institutions, especially under the Bush administration. But robust U.S. leadership is sine qua non to constructive relations among major powers, and to the future relevance and workability of international institutions such as the WTO, International Monetary Fund, and World Bank. They would be lame and sidelined without it.

More crucial than ever will be U.S. relations with the rising powers of Asia-Pacific, China and India. Here there are welcome trends. Both the Clinton and the Bush administrations have pursued "constructive engagement" with China and India, largely driven by deepening commercial links. But this is frequently thrown off balance by protectionist pressures and foreign policy hawks who wish to "contain" rather than "engage" China in particular. It is vital that these forces are contained so that constructive engagement can continue. This will, in turn, reinforce positive foreign policy trends in China and India.

What about foreign policy in China and India? The imperatives of China's modern foreign policy are steady integration into the global economy and political stability in the East Asian neighborhood. These objectives have driven fundamental change in China's relations with other major powers, and its participation in international institutions. Constructive engagement characterizes China's key bilateral relationships and its role in international institutions. Trade diplomacy, multilaterally in the WTO and on bilateral and regional tracks, is perhaps the most visible sign of this foreign policy transformation.

Set against these very real trends, however, are occasional tendencies of aggressive nationalism. This seems to be directed at Taiwan and Japan, notwithstanding ever-closer commercial ties with them. Finally, the Chinese government seems happy to maintain cozy relations with some of the most repulsive regimes around the world—not least with African governments in the scramble to secure energy supplies. An optimist would argue that foreign policy will ultimately be swayed by the imperatives of global economic integration. Optimism, however, should always be tinged with realism.

India's foreign policy has undergone a parallel transformation since the end of the cold war. It has switched from leadership of the "non-aligned" Third World and support for the Soviet Union to constructive engagement with other powers in the developed and developing worlds. Its relations with the United States are blossoming, on both the high politics of security and the low politics of commercial relations. It is playing a more forward-looking, system-maintaining—rather than system-wrecking—game in international institutions. However, this has not yet translated into much more pragmatic and flexible diplomacy in the WTO—one key difference with China.

Conclusion

Throughout this book, I have argued that the impulse for freer trade does not and will not come from international institutions. Global-governance chatter and blueprints are mere flatulence and fluff. Rather, the liberalization impulse comes and will come from national governance and unilateral example setting, especially from Asia and from China in particular. A serviceable multilateralism is important, especially in the WTO. But that can happen only with suitably modest and realistic goals and instruments. Finally, enlightened U.S. leadership and constructive engagement among major powers are the requisites for the preservation of the global Pax.

Asia's transformation of the world economy holds out huge opportunities for growth, poverty reduction, improvements in human welfare, and the extension of economic freedoms. Not least, it will contribute to peaceful international relations as nations and peoples come closer together through commercial ties. For the first time in world history, it is Asia, not the West, that represents the best hope for the free-trade trinity of prosperity, freedom, and peace. That has profound political and economic ramifications.

More generally, liberal optimists would conclude that global prospects today look a lot better than they did a century ago. Interstate political and military rivalry today is low-grade compared with pre–World War I jingoism. Post-1945 globalization has created powerful commercial interests with strong stakes in open markets. New Millennium Collectivism is not as noxious as the deadly ideological combination of nationalism and socialism in the first half of the 20th century.[19]

But nothing is preprogrammed—the eternal lesson of summer 1914. The magnitude of unfolding changes in the global economy is bound to increase protectionist pressures, in developed and developing countries. Governments, not least in China and India, have to manage internal problems, such as rising regional disparities, rotting public sectors, environmental pollution, corruption, and anxiety about health, education, and pensions systems among the most vulnerable. Then there is the problematic link between a spreading market economy and authoritarian politics, particularly in China. Finally, there are international security flashpoints, such as China-Taiwan and China-Japan relations, China's growing military power in east Asia, and the big-power scramble for global energy supplies— not to mention Islamic fundamentalism, international terrorism, rogue states, and failed states. All these could slow down or even halt the onward march of global economic integration.

Good management of international economic policy requires what Martin Wolf calls "liberal realism": maintaining a balance between power politics and cooperation in international institutions; working with the grain of outward-looking commercial interests (such as exporters, downstream users of imported inputs, multinational firms with global production networks, and cities and regions seeking to attract FDI) that can counter inward-looking protectionist interests; and taking advantage of (often unanticipated) events.

Ideas also have their place in this scheme, and they are not to be underestimated. That is why I have made the case for free trade in a classical-liberal, limited-government, laissez faire framework—and not as part of a social democracy I find mealy-mouthed, internally contradictory, and not well fitted for 21st-century globalization. The idea of free trade now lacks the commanding champions it once had—the likes of mid-Victorian titans such as Peel, Gladstone, Cobden, and Bright, or 20th-century equivalents such as Cordell Hull and Ludwig Erhard. To repeat John Stuart Mill's felicitous words: it is "the word in season, which, at a critical moment, does much to decide the result." Thus, it falls to free trade's friends to spread their word *in season with* the global political and economic currents of the new century.

Notes

Chapter 2

1. This section draws on Jacob Viner's brilliant Wabash lectures. These wonderful miniatures are found in J. Viner, *Essays on the Intellectual History of Economics*, ed. D. A. Irwin (Princeton, NJ: Princeton University Press, 1991), pp. 39–81. Also see D. A. Irwin, *Against the Tide: An Intellectual History of Free Trade* (Princeton, NJ: Princeton University Press, 1996), chap. 1.

2. C. Hull, "The True Nature of Trade," in *The Memoirs of Cordell Hull* (New York: Macmillan, 1948), p. 81.

3. This section draws on Irwin, *Against the Tide*, chap. 2; Viner, *Essays*, pp. 262–76; and J. A. Schumpeter, *History of Economic Analysis* (London: Routledge, 1950), pp. 335–78.

4. Quoted in L. Robbins, *A History of Economic Thought: The LSE Lectures*, ed. S. Medema and W. Samuels (Princeton, NJ: Princeton University Press, 1998), p. 52.

5. This section draws on Irwin, *Against the Tide*, chaps. 3 and 4.

6. Quoted in ibid., p. 54.

7. A. Smith, *An Inquiry into the Nature and Causes of the Wealth of Nations*. 1776, ed. E. Cannan (Chicago: University of Chicago Press, 1976), book 4, chap. 9, p. 208.

8. See D. Hume, "Of the Jealousy of Trade," in *Writings on Economics (1758)*, ed. E. Rotwein (Madison: University of Wisconsin Press, 1970).

9. This section draws especially on R. Sally, *Classical Liberalism and International Economic Order: Studies in Theory and Intellectual History* (London: Routledge, 1998), chap. 3. Also see Irwin, *Against the Tide*, chap. 5; Robbins, *A History of Economic Thought*, Lectures 11–16; Schumpeter, *History of Economic Analysis*, pp. 181–94; and Viner, *Essays*, chaps. 2 and 10.

10. Quoted in Hume, "Of the Jealousy of Trade," pp. 78, 82.

11. Quoted in Smith, *The Wealth of Nations*, book 4, chap. 3, p. 519.

12. See Hla Myint's brilliant essays on Adam Smith's theory of external trade and its link to development, especially "The 'Classical Theory' of International Trade and the Underdeveloped Countries," *Economic Journal* 68 (1958): 317–37; and "Adam Smith's Theory of International Trade in the Perspective of Economic Development," *Economica* 44 (1977): 231–48.

13. Smith, *The Wealth of Nations*, book 4, chap. 2, p. 494, and chap. 3, p. 518.

14. L. Robbins, *Robert Torrens and the Evolution of Classical Economics* (London: Macmillan, 1958), p. 255.

15. See L. Robbins, *Economic Planning and International Order* (London: Macmillan, 1936); and F. A. Hayek, *The Road to Serfdom* (London: Routledge, 1944), pp. 163–76.

16. This section draws on Irwin, *Against the Tide*, chaps. 6, 7, and 8; Robbins, *A History of Economic Thought*, Lectures 17–25; Schumpeter, *History of Economic Analysis*, part 3, chaps. 2–5; and J. Viner, *Studies in the Theory of International Trade* (London:

George Allen and Unwin, 1937). Also see A. Howe, *Free Trade and Liberal England, 1846–1946* (Oxford: Clarendon, 1997).

17. Quoted in Irwin, *Against the Tide*, p. 114.

18. Schumpeter, *History of Economic Analysis*, p. 398.

19. This section draws on Irwin, *Against the Tide*, chaps. 12–15; J. Bhagwati, *Free Trade Today* (Princeton, NJ: Princeton University Press, 2002); and D. Lal, *Reviving the Invisible Hand: The Case for Classical Liberalism in the Twenty-First Century* (Princeton, NJ: Princeton University Press, 2006), chaps. 1–3.

20. Viner, *Theory of International Trade*, p. 298.

21. Quoted in Irwin, *Against the Tide*, p. 199.

22. See Lal, *Reviving the Invisible Hand*, chap. 3. Also see B. Lindsey, *Against the Dead Hand: The Uncertain Struggle for Global Capitalism* (Washington, DC: John Wiley, 2002).

Chapter 3

1. See J. Stiglitz, *Globalisation and Its Discontents* (London: Allen Lane, 2002); H. J. Chang, *Kicking Away the Ladder: Development Strategy in Historical Perspective* (London: Anthem Press, 2002); I. Grunberg, I. Kaul, and M. Stern, eds., *Global International Goods: International Co-Operation in the 21st Century* (New York and Oxford: Oxford University Press, 1999); Oxfam, *Rigged Rules and Double Standards: Trade, Globalisation and the Fight against Poverty* (Oxford: Oxfam International, 2002), www.marketrade-fair.com; D. Rodrik, "Trading in Illusions," *Foreign Policy* (March/April 2001), www.foreignpolicy.com/issue_marapr_2001/rodrick.html; and J. Sachs, *The End of Poverty: How We Can Make It Happen in Our Lifetime* (London: Penguin, 2005).

2. J. Bhagwati and T. N. Srinivasan, "Outward-Orientation and Development: Are Revisionists Right?" Yale University Economic Growth Center Discussion Paper 806, 1999; D. Lal and H. Myint, *The Political Economy of Poverty, Equity and Growth: A Comparative Study* (Oxford: Clarendon Press, 1996).

3. See, for example, J. Sachs and A. Warner, "Economic Reform and the Process of Global Integration," *Brookings Papers on Economic Activity* 1 (1995): 1–118; A. L. Winters, "Trade Liberalisation and Economic Performance: An Overview," *Economic Journal* 114 (2004): F4–F21; and A. L. Winters, "Trade Liberalisation and Poverty," *Journal of Economic Literature* 42 (2004): 72–115.

4. World Bank, *Globalisation, Growth and Poverty: Building an Inclusive World Economy* (Washington, DC: World Bank, 2002), p. 34, especially table 1.1; Maddison, *The World Economy: Historical Statistics* (Paris: OECD, 2003).

5. M. Wolf, *Why Globalization Works: The Case for the Global Market Economy* (New Haven, CT: Yale University Press, 2004), chap. 9; D. Henderson, "Globalisation, Economic Progress and New Millennium Collectivism," *World Economics* 5 (2004): 52–58.

6. Oxfam, *Rigged Rules and Double Standards*; M. D. Ingco and J. D. Nash, eds., *Agriculture and the WTO: Creating a Trading System for Development* (Washington, DC: World Bank, 2004).

7. World Bank, *The East Asian Miracle* (Washington, DC: World Bank, 1993); I. M. D. Little, "Trade and Industrialisation Revisited," in *Collection and Recollections*, ed. I. M. D. Little (Oxford: Clarendon, 1999).

8. D. Henderson, "International Economic Integration: Progress, Prospects and Implications," *International Affairs* 64 (1992): 635.

9. On the record of trade and FDI liberalization as part of larger packages of market-based reforms in developing countries and countries in transition, see J.

Williamson, ed., *The Political Economy of Policy Reform* (Washington, DC: Institute for International Economics, 1993); P. P. Kuczynski and J. Williamson, eds., *After the Washington Consensus: Restarting Growth and Reform in Latin America* (Washington, DC: Institute for International Economics, 2004); Lal and Myint, *Political Economy of Poverty, Equity and Growth*; J. Dean, "The Trade-Policy Revolution in Developing Countries," *World Economy, Global Trade Policy* 18, no. 5 (Fall 1995): 173–90. Z. Drabek and S. Laird, "The New Liberalism: Trade-Policy Developments in Emerging Markets," *Journal of World Trade* 32 (1998): 241–69; D. Henderson, *The Changing Fortunes of Economic Liberalism: Yesterday, Today and Tomorrow* (London: Institute of Economic Affairs, 1998); and C. Michalopoulos, *Developing Countries and the WTO* (London: Palgrave, 2001). On trade-policy trends in Asia, see R. Sally, "Trade Policy in Asia," ECIPE Policy Brief 1, www.ecipe.org/pdf/Policybrief_0107.pdf; R. Sally, "Chinese Trade Policies in Wider Asian Perspective," in *Globalisation and Economic Growth in China*, ed. Y. Yao and L. Yueh (London: World Scientific Publishing, 2006), pp. 181–233; and R. Sally and R. Sen, "Whither Trade Policies in Southeast Asia? The Wider Asian and Global Context," *ASEAN Economic Bulletin* 22 (2005): 92–115 (including individual country papers in special issue on revisiting trade policies in southeast Asia).

10. S. Haggard and J. Williamson, "The Political Conditions for Economic Reform," in *The Political Economy of Policy Reform*, ed. J. Williamson (Washington, DC: Institute for International Economics, 1993), pp. 527–96; L. Balcerowicz, *Socialism, Capitalism, Transformation* (Budapest: Central European University Press, 1995).

11. M. Olson, *The Logic of Collective Action: Public Goods and the Theory of Groups* (Cambridge, MA: Harvard University Press, 1971); A. O. Krueger, "The Political Economy of the Rent-Seeking Society," *American Economic Review* 64 (1974): 291–303.

12. Ricardo-Viner and Hecksher-Ohlin models of comparative advantage are used to explain interest-group activity pro and contra free trade in different countries with different factor endowments. See J. Frieden and R. Rogowski, "The Impact of the International Economy on National Policies," in *Internationalisation and Domestic Politics*, ed. R. Keohane and H. Milner (Cambridge: Cambridge University Press, 1996), pp. 25–47; and R. Rogowski, *Commerce and Coalitions: How Trade Affects Domestic Political Alignments* (Princeton, NJ: Princeton University Press, 1990).

13. On "ideational" approaches, see J. Goldstein, *Ideas, Interests and American Trade Policy* (Ithaca, NY: Cornell University Press, 1994).

14. P. T. Bauer, ed., *From Subsistence to Exchange and Other Essays* (Princeton, NJ: Princeton University Press, 2000); Lal and Myint, *The Political Economy of Poverty, Equity and Growth*.

15. See the World Bank's governance and business climate indicators. They point to large institutional and policy differences among developing countries. They also point to relatively weak institutions, as well as the high "red tape" costs of doing business, in China and India. World Bank, *Doing Business in 2007* (Washington, DC: World Bank, 2006); World Bank governance indicators, www.worldbank.org.

16. In *The Political Economy of Poverty, Equity and Growth*, Lal and Myint provide perhaps the best analysis of how factor endowments have influenced the political economy of postcolonial policy reforms in developing countries.

17. Wolf, *Why Globalization Works*.

18. There is the theoretical possibility of (usually large) countries being able to exercise long-run market power in international demand for certain goods. This enables them to shift the terms of trade in their favor by means of an "optimal tariff." The corollary is that these countries should lower tariffs only if others reciprocate,

to avoid worsening terms of trade. In reality, very few countries have such long-run market power. And retaliatory tariffs by other countries could nullify terms-of-trade gains. Thus—not for the first time—a neat theory turns out to have limited practical relevance. See D. A. Irwin, *Against the Tide: An Intellectual History of Free Trade* (Princeton, NJ: Princeton University Press, 1996), pp. 106–15.

19. World Bank, *Global Economic Prospects 2005: Trade, Regionalism and Development* (Washington, DC: World Bank/OUP, 2004).

20. This section draws on F. Erixon and R. Sally, "Trade and Aid: Countering New Millennium Collectivism," Australian Economic Review 39 (2006): 69–77.

21. World Bank, *1998 Annual Review of Development Effectiveness* (Washington, DC: Operations Evaluation Department, World Bank, 1998); World Bank, *Assessing Aid: What Works, What Doesn't, and Why* (Oxford: Oxford University Press, 1998).

22. P. T. Bauer, "Foreign Aid: Abiding Issues," in *From Subsistence to Exchange and Other Essays*, ed. P. T. Bauer (Princeton, NJ: Princeton University Press, 2000).

23. UN Millennium Project, *Investing in Development: A Practical Plan to Achieve the Millennium Development Goals* (New York: Earthscan, 2005); Sachs, *The End of Poverty*.

24. W. Easterly, *The White Man's Burden: Why the West's Efforts to Aid the Rest Have Done So Much Ill and So Little Good* (New York: Penguin, 2006).

25. World Bank, *Assessing Aid*.

26. M. Olson, *The Rise and Decline of Nations: Economic Growth, Stagflation and Social Rigidities* (New Haven, CT: Yale University Press, 1982); OECD, *Economic Policy Reforms: Going for Growth* (Paris: OECD, 2007).

27. World Bank, *Doing Business in 2007*. See also World Bank governance indicators, www.worldbank.org.

28. P. Messerlin, *Europe after the "No" Votes: Mapping a New Economic Path* (London: Institute of Economic Affairs, 2006).

29. Ibid. This is the headline objective of the European Centre for International Political Economy, the new Brussels-based think tank I run with Fredrik Erixon. See our mission statement at www.ecipe.org.

30. On the provenance and progress of these ideas, see D. Henderson, *Anti-Liberalism 2000: The Rise of New Millennium Collectivism* (London: Institute of Economic Affairs, 2001).

Chapter 4

1. J. Bhagwati, *Free Trade Today* (Princeton, NJ: Princeton University Press, 2002), pp. 51–52, 67.

2. C. Barfield, *Free Trade, Sovereignty, Democracy: The Future of the World Trade Organization* (Washington, DC: American Enterprise Institute, 2001).

3. "Declaration on the TRIPS Agreement and Public Health," WT/MIN(01)/DEC/W/2, WTO, Geneva, 2001, www.wto.org; "Implementation-Related Issues and Concerns," WT/MIN(01)/W/10, WTO, 2001,www.wto.org; "Ministerial Declaration," WT/MIN(01)/DEC/W/1, WTO, 2001, www.wto.org.

4. "Ministerial Declaration" and "Ministerial Declaration: Annexes," WT/MIN(05)/DEC, WTO, Geneva, 2005, www.wto.org/english/thewto_e/minist_e/min05_e/final_text_e.htm.

5. This is the gist of a recent think piece by Simon Evenett. See S. Evenett "EU Commercial Policy in a Multipolar Trading System," 2007. Copy in author's files.

6. Counting the EU as 1, and stripping out intra-EU trade, 10 countries make up about 70 percent of world trade.

7. See D. Esty, "The World Trade Organisation's Legitimacy Crisis," *World Trade Review* 1 (2002): 7–22.

8. Many of these barbarians are also middle-class fakes who flit from conference to workshop around the world presuming to speak on behalf of the poor and oppressed. Funding from aid agencies, that is, Western taxpayers, keeps the circus on the road. These types remind me of Paul Theroux's acid description of aid workers as "joy-riding agents of virtue . . . oafish, self-dramatising prigs and, often, complete bastards." They fit Tom Wolfe's "radical-chic" category, full of *nostalgie de la boue* ("nostalgia for the mud," i.e., romanticizing the primitive and excoriating everything middle class). The species also reminds me of a Western interloper who figures in V. S. Naipaul's reportage on the Black Power movement in the Caribbean: "Benson was as shallow and vain and parasitic as many middle-class dropouts of her time . . . the people who substitute doctrine for knowledge and irritation for concern, the revolutionaries who visit centres of revolution with return air tickets, the hippies, the people who wish themselves on societies more fragile than their own." V. S. Naipaul, "Papa and the Power Set," in *The Writer and the World: Essays*, ed. V. S. Naipaul (London: Picador, 2004). Also see P. Theroux, *Dark Star Safari* (London: Penguin, 2003); and T. Wolfe, *Radical Chic and Mau-Mauing the Flak Catchers* (New York: Farrer, Strauss, and Giroux, 1970).

9. Rules of the classical-liberal type, in the tradition from Hume and Smith to Hayek and Tumlir, are general rules of conduct, applying equally to all, which are negative (or proscriptive) in the sense that they tell actors what not to do, but otherwise leave them free to do as they wish. They should be distinguished from specific, prescriptive regulations, which usually involve executive discretion and fall within the sphere of public administrative law. See R. Sally, *Classical Liberalism and International Economic Order: Studies in Theory and Intellectual History* (London: Routledge, 1998), pp. 26–28, 115ff.

10. J. Tumlir, "International Economic Order and Democratic Constitutionalism," *Ordo* 34 (1983): 72.

11. As Fareed Zakaria puts it: "If trade negotiators allowed for constant democratic input, they [WTO agreements] would be riddled with exceptions, caveats, and shields for politically powerful groups. . . . More democracy in trade policy would mean more policies like agricultural subsidies. . . . The world has made more economic progress in the last fifty years than in the previous five hundred. Do we really want to destroy the system that made this happen by making it [the WTO] function like the California legislature?" F. Zakaria, *The Future of Democracy: Illiberal Democracy at Home and Abroad* (New York: W. W. Norton, 2003), p. 246.

12. M. Wolf, *Why Globalisation Works: The Case for the Global Market Economy* (New Haven, CT: Yale University Press, 2004), p. 295.

Chapter 5

1. In FTAs, members remove tariff and nontariff barriers between themselves but retain separate trade policies with respect to third countries. Members of a customs union have a common external tariff for third-country imports. Partial-scope agreements are between developing countries and have limited product coverage. They are usually notified under the GATT's enabling clause. FTAs and customs unions

are supposed to be comprehensive in scope and conform to the provisions of GATT Article XXIV ("substantially all trade" in goods) and General Agreement on Trade in Services Article V ("substantial sectoral coverage" in services).

2. "Regional Trade Agreements: Facts and Figures," WTO, Geneva, 2007, www.wto.org/english/tratop_e/region_e/regfac_e.htm; J. A. Crawford and R. V. Fiorentino, "The Changing Landscape of Regional Trade Agreements," WTO Discussion Paper 8, 2005, www.wto.org.

3. R. Sen,"'New Regionalism' in Asia: A Comparative Analysis of Emerging Regional and Bilateral Trading Agreements Involving ASEAN, China and India," *Journal of World Trade* 40 (2006): 553–96; S. Evenett, ed., "The European Union's New Trade Policy," Special Issue, *Aussenwirtschaft* 61 (2006): 377–402.

4. A "duckspeaker" is someone whose speech emerges mechanically from the larynx without engaging the higher brain cells. See G. Orwell, "1984," in *George Orwell: The Complete Novels* (Penguin, London, 2000), p. 923.

5. The following account on PTA motives, advantages, and disadvantages draws on World Bank, "Regional Trade Agreements and Development: Upside Potential and Downside Risks," Trade Note 24, September 13, 2005, http://siteresources. worldbank.org/INTRANETTRADE/Resources/239054-1126812419270/TradeNote24_ Newfarmer.pdf; and World Bank, *Global Economic Prospects 2005: Trade, Regionalism and Development* (Washington, DC: World Bank/OUP, 2004).

6. Rules to determine the country of origin of a good do not matter if there are zero tariffs, and matter little if trade takes place on a nondiscriminatory (most favored nation) basis, as it is supposed to do in the GATT/WTO. But such rules do matter for PTAs, as they determine whether a good qualifies for duty-free or preferential-tariff entry to the market of a PTA member.

7. "Rules-of-Origin Regimes in Regional Trade Agreements," Background survey by the Secretariat, Committee on Regional Trade Agreements, WT/REG/W/45, WTO, Geneva, April 5, 2003, www.wto.org; A. Estevadeordal and K. Suominen, "Rules of Origin in the World Trading System," (paper prepared for the seminar on regional trade agreements and the WTO), World Trade Organization, Washington, DC, November 14, 2003.

8. This section draws on R. Sally, "FTAs and the Prospects for Regional Integration in Asia," ECIPE Working Paper 1, 2006, www.ecipe.org/publications/2006/WPno1_ 06_Sally.pdf. Also see A. Antkiewicz and J. Whalley, "China's New Regional Trade Agreements," *World Economy* 28 (2005): 1540, 1554–55; R. Baldwin, "Implications of European Experiences with Regionalism for Future Economic Integration in Asia," 2006. Copy in author's files; R. Baldwin, "Multilateralising Regionalism: Spaghetti Bowls as Building Blocs on the Path to Global Free Trade," *World Economy* 29 (2006): 1451–1518; and H. Soesastro, "Regional Integration in East Asia: Achievements and Future Prospects," *Asian Economic Policy Review* 1 (2006): 215–34.

9. See C. F. Bergsten, "Toward a Free Trade Area of the Asia Pacific," Policy Briefs in International Economics, No. PB07-2, Peterson Institute for International Economics, Washington, DC, February 2007, www.petersoninstitute.org.

10. Also see P. Athukorala, "Product Fragmentation and Trade Patterns in East Asia," *Asian Economic Papers* 4 (2006): 1–27.

11. Baldwin, "Multilateralising Regionalism," pp. 1451–1518.

12. P. Sutherland et al., *The Future of the WTO: Addressing Institutional Challenges in the New Millennium* (Geneva: WTO, 2005).

Chapter 6

1. R. Axelrod and R. O. Keohane, "Achieving Co-operation under Anarchy," in *Neorealism and Neoliberalism: The Contemporary Debate*, ed. D. Baldwin (New York: Columbia University Press, 1993), p. 109. Also see R. O. Keohane, *After Hegemony: Co-operation and Discord in the World Political Economy* (Princeton, NJ: Princeton University Press, 1984); and R. O. Keohane, "Reciprocity in International Relations," *International Organisation* 40 (1986): 1–27.

2. J. Tumlir, "Need for an Open Multilateral Trading System," *The World Economy* 6 (1983): 400.

3. J. Tumlir, "International Economic Order and Democratic Constitutionalism," *Ordo* 34 (1983): 76–77.

4. World Bank, "Regional Trade Agreements and Development: Upside Potential and Downside Risks," Trade Note 24, September 13, 2005, p. 5, http://sitere sources.worldbank.org/INTRANETTRADE/Resources/239054-1126812419270/ TradeNote24_Newfarmer.pdf.

5. This section draws on R. Sally, "Chinese Trade Policies in Wider Asian Perspective," in *Globalisation and Economic Growth in China*, ed. Y. Yao and L. Yueh (London: World Scientific Publishing, 2006), pp. 181–233.

6. G. Myrdal, *Asian Drama: An Inquiry into the Poverty of Nations*, 3 vols. (London: Harmondsworth/Penguin, 1968).

7. For an excellent shorthand account of Asia's role in the world economy, see Martin Wolf's columns in the *Financial Times*, for example, "Why Europe Was the Past, the US Is the Present and a China-Dominated Asia the Future of the Global Economy," September 22, 2003; "Three Reasons to Be Cheerful about the World Economy," June 30, 2004; "On the Move: Asia's Giants Take Different Routes in Pursuit of Economic Greatness," February 23, 2005; "What India Must Do to Outpace China," February 14, 2006; "Answer to Asia's Rise Is Not to Retreat," March 14, 2006; and "China Should Stick to Trial and Error—But Risk Bolder Trials," June 7, 2006.

8. I am grateful to Roderick Abbott for these estimates, calculated from *International Trade Statistics 2005* (Geneva: WTO, 2006). All figures and rankings exclude intra-EU trade.

9. See R. Sally and R. Sen, "Whither Trade Policies in Southeast Asia? The Wider Asian and Global Context," *ASEAN Economic Bulletin* 22 (2005): 92–115, and individual country papers, in Special Issue on Revisiting Trade Policies in Southeast Asia, *ASEAN Economic Bulletin* 22 (2005).

10. N. Lardy, *Integrating China into the Global Economy* (Washington, DC: Brookings Institution, 2002).

11. See WTO, "Rules-of-Origin Regimes in Regional Trade Agreements," background survey by the Secretariat, Committee on Regional Trade Agreements, WT/ REG/W/45, April 5, 2003, www.wto.org; E. Ianchovichina and W. Martin, "Trade Liberalization in China's Accession to the World Trade Organization," Policy Research Working Paper 2623, World Bank, Washington, DC, 2001, http://www.world-bank.org; A. Mattoo, "China's Accession to the WTO: The Services Dimension," *Journal of International Economic Law* 6 (2003): 299–339; and D. Bhattasali, L. Shantong, and W. Martin, *China's Accession to the World Trade Organisation, Policy Reform and Poverty Reduction* (Washington, DC: World Bank, 2004).

12. "Trade Policy Review: India 2007," Document WT/TPR/S/182, WTO, Geneva, April 18, 2007, http://64.233.169.104/search?q=cache:cctu5slYwz4J:www.wto.org/ english/tratop_e/tpr_e/s182-00_e.doc+/WT/TPR/S/182&hl=en&ct=clnk&cd=

1&gl = us; A. Mattoo and R. Stern, eds., *India and the WTO* (Washington, DC: World Bank/OUP, 2003).

13. R. Baldwin, "Implications of European Experiences with Regionalism for Future Economic Integration in Asia," 2006. Copy in author's files; R. Baldwin, "Multilateralising Regionalism: Spaghetti Bowls as Building Blocs on the Path to Global Free Trade," *The World Economy* 29 (2006): 1451–1518; P. Athukorala, "Product Fragmentation and Trade Patterns in East Asia," *Asian Economic Papers* 4 (2006): 1–27.

14. This is the coda to Deputy Secretary of State Robert Zoellick's much-publicized speech on U.S.-China relations. It is also the underlying logic of the U.S.-China Strategic Economic Dialogue, established in late 2006 following the initiative of U.S. Treasury Secretary Hank Paulson. R. Zoellick, "Whither China: From Membership to Responsibility?" Speech on U.S.-China relations and remarks to the National Committee on U.S.-China Relations, New York, September 21, 2005, www.state.gov/s/d/former/zoellick/rem/53682.htm.

15. W. Röpke, *International Order and Economic Integration* (Dordrecht, Neth.: Reidel, 1959), pp. 9–20.

Chapter 7

1. The concept of international trade as a handmaiden of growth comes from Irving Kravis. See I. Kravis, "Trade as a Handmaiden of Growth: Similarities between the Nineteenth and Twentieth Centuries," *Economic Journal* 80 (1970): 850–72.

2. D. Lal, *Unintended Consequences: The Impact of Factor Endowments, Culture and Politics on Long-Run Economic Performance* (Cambridge, MA: MIT Press, 1998).

3. P. T. Bauer, "Western Guilt and Third World Poverty," in *From Subsistence to Exchange and Other Essays*, ed. P. T. Bauer (Princeton, NJ: Princeton University Press, 2000), pp. 57–59.

4. See Martin Wolf's recent columns on the issue in the *Financial Times*: "Confronting Seismic Economic Shifts," January 31, 2006; "A New Gilded Age," April 25, 2006; and "A Divided World of Economic Success and Political Turmoil," January 30, 2007; and *The Economist*'s article "The New Titans," September 14, 2006.

5. A. Beattie, "Avoiding the Crush," *Financial Times*, June 14, 2007.

6. See Lawrence Summers's columns in the *Financial Times*: "The Global Middle Class Cries Out for Reassurance," October 29, 2006; "Lack of Fear Gives Cause for Concern," December 26, 2006; and "Harnessing Market Forces to Share Prosperity," June 24, 2007.

7. The perpetual caricature of classical liberalism is that it supports a night watchman state, a "harmony-of-interests" doctrine, and anarcho-capitalist laissez faire. That is rubbish. Hume, Smith, John Stuart Mill, Alfred Marshall, F. A. Hayek, and others in the tradition never held these views. See R. Sally, *Classical Liberalism and International Economic Order: Studies in Theory and Intellectual History* (London: Routledge, 1998), chap. 2.

8. P. Legrain, *Immigrants: Your Country Needs Them* (London: Little Brown, 2006).

9. P. Seabright, *The Company of Strangers* (Princeton, NJ: Princeton University Press, 2004).

10. P. Collier, *The Bottom Billion* (Oxford: Oxford University Press, 2007).

11. J. Bhagwati, *Free Trade Today* (Princeton, NJ: Princeton University Press, 2002), pp. 52–57.

12. D. Henderson, *Misguided Virtue: False Notions of Corporate Social Responsibility* (London: Institute of Economic Affairs, 2004).

13. J. S. Mill, *Autobiography*, 1873 (London: Penguin Classics, 1989), p. 179.

14. Hayek's views apropos are most comprehensively set out in F. A. Hayek, *The Road to Serfdom* (London: Routledge, 1944); and F. A. Hayek, *Law, Legislation and Liberty* (London: Routledge, 1982). The distinction between economic process and economic order comes from Walter Eucken, one of the founders of the Freiburg School of Ordoliberalism. See Sally, *Classical Liberalism and International Economic Order*, chap. 6.

15. M. Oakeshott, *Morality and Politics in Modern Europe: The Harvard Lectures* (New Haven, CT: Yale University Press, 1993), pp. 47–58, 100–10.

16. J. Tumlir, "National Sovereignty, Power and Interest," *Ordo* 31 (1980): 3; J. Tumlir, "International Economic Order and Democratic Constitutionalism," *Ordo* 34 (1983): 72; Sally, *Classical Liberalism and International Economic Order*, chap. 8.

17. For a representative view, see I. Grunberg, I. Kaul, and M. Stern, eds., *Global International Goods: International Co-Operation in the 21st Century* (New York and Oxford: Oxford University Press, 1999).

18. There are exceptions to such a generalization. First, the European Union has substantial supranational competence, especially in relations with third countries. But the European Union is sui generis. Second, failed and failing states do not provide, or hardly provide, the core functions mentioned. These, however, are the exceptions, not the rule.

19. M. Wolf, *Why Globalisation Works: The Case for the Global Market Economy* (New Haven, CT: Yale University Press, 2004), pp. 308–13.

Index

Page references followed by t or f
denote tables or figures, respectively.

Africa
  factor endowments, 42
  free trade agreements, 46
  infant industry protection, 26
  liberalization, 35, 44
  preferential trade agreements, 79, 80f
  reform fatigue, 23
Africa Commission, 47
agricultural liberalization, 25
agricultural protection, Japan and
    South Korea, 82
agricultural protectionism, 22
agricultural subsidies, 64, 78, 79
aid-to-reform and "aid-for-trade"
    scheme, 47–48
anti-dumping, 26, 28, 28f, 51, 78, 79
anti-liberalization ideas, 48
Argentina
  economic crisis, 37
  factor endowments, 42
  liberalization, 35
Aristotle, 6
ASEAN (Association of Southeast
    Asian Nations)
  economic summit participation, 88
  "Factory Asia" phenomenon, 101, 107
  preferential trade agreements, 75, 76,
    82–83. See also specific countries
  regional economic integration
    initiatives, 86–90
ASEAN Free Trade Area, 80
Asia
  Asian financial crises, 23
  division of labor, 101–2, 120
  economic and trade indicators, 99,
    100t
  globalization, 24–25, 96–102, 110–14,
    118, 120–26
  implications for Asia in WTO, 88–89
  indicators for trade across borders,
    112t
  liberalization impulse, 133

nationalist rivalry, 88
percentile world rank of governance
    indicators, 113t
post-Doha reforms, 109–10
preferential trade agreements, 82–86
trade policy reforms, 96–97, 102–8,
    120–26, 133
world gross domestic product and,
    97–99, 98f, 99f
world ranking in ease of doing
    business, 111t
See also specific countries and regions
Asia-Pacific Economic Cooperation
  regional economic integration
    initiatives, 86–88
Asian Drama, 96
Association of Southeast Asian
    Nations. See ASEAN (Association
    of Southeast Asian Nations)
Australia
  economic crisis, 37
  factor endowments, 42
  liberalization, 35
  preferential trade agreements, 75
  unilateral tariff liberalization, 45
Australian Productivity Commission,
    51
Australia–New Zealand Closer
    Economic Relations Trade
    Agreement, 78
Axelrod, Robert, 92

Baldwin, Richard, 87
Baltic States
  economic crisis, 38
  liberalization, 35
barriers to trade
  nontariff barriers in developing
    countries, 32, 33t, 63, 82, 102–5,
    104t
  regulatory, 29, 49–50, 78, 84, 102–5,
    110
Bay of Bengal Initiative for Multi-
    Sectoral Technical and Economic
    Cooperation, 85

About the Author

Razeen Sally is director of the European Centre for International Political Economy, an international economic policy think tank based in Brussels, and is on the faculty of the London School of Economics. His research focuses on international trade policy, especially in Asia, and on the intellectual history of political economy. He writes and comments widely on international economic issues and spends much of his time working and traveling in east and south Asia. He is on the advisory board of the Cato Center for Trade Policy Studies.

Cato Institute

Founded in 1977, the Cato Institute is a public policy research foundation dedicated to broadening the parameters of policy debate to allow consideration of more options that are consistent with the traditional American principles of limited government, individual liberty, and peace. To that end, the Institute strives to achieve greater involvement of the intelligent, concerned lay public in questions of policy and the proper role of government.

The Institute is named for *Cato's Letters*, libertarian pamphlets that were widely read in the American Colonies in the early 18th century and played a major role in laying the philosophical foundation for the American Revolution.

Despite the achievement of the nation's Founders, today virtually no aspect of life is free from government encroachment. A pervasive intolerance for individual rights is shown by government's arbitrary intrusions into private economic transactions and its disregard for civil liberties.

To counter that trend, the Cato Institute undertakes an extensive publications program that addresses the complete spectrum of policy issues. Books, monographs, and shorter studies are commissioned to examine the federal budget, Social Security, regulation, military spending, international trade, and myriad other issues. Major policy conferences are held throughout the year, from which papers are published thrice yearly in the *Cato Journal*. The Institute also publishes the quarterly magazine *Regulation*.

In order to maintain its independence, the Cato Institute accepts no government funding. Contributions are received from foundations, corporations, and individuals, and other revenue is generated from the sale of publications. The Institute is a nonprofit, tax-exempt, educational foundation under Section 501(c)3 of the Internal Revenue Code.

CATO INSTITUTE
1000 Massachusetts Ave., N.W.
Washington, D.C. 20001
www.cato.org